No Way to Treat a Lady ...

Edge squeezed the triggers of both guns simultaneously and shot Arnie and John in their chests as they made to swing their guns toward him. Heart shots, the bullets tearing through flesh and passing between lower ribs on a rising trajectory to penetrate the vital organs. Not bringing death to the victims until they had a second in which to realize it was the end for them.

The elder man, who received the revolver bullet, simply straightened up, swayed to the side, and fell, firing his gun at the ground in front of him. The higher velocity of the bullet from the Winchester lifted the other man an inch or so off the ground and hurled him violently backward. He tried to bring his hands up to the blossoming stain on his shirt front, but never made it. His gun fell from his nerveless grasp without being fired.

Edge swung up the rifle to his left shoulder. He had the revolver hammer thumbed back and the gun aimed at Fay's baby-doll face.

"You wouldn't shoot a lady, would you, mister?" she asked.

THE EDGE SERIES:

#40

EDGE

MONTANA MELODRAMA

BY

George G. Gilman

PINNACLE BOOKS   NEW YORK

EDGE #40: MONTANA MELODRAMA

Copyright © 1981 by George G. Gilman

A Pinnacle Book. First published in Great Britain by New English Library Ltd., 1981.

First printing, July 1982

ISBN: 0-523-41451-X

Cover illustration by Bruce Minney

Printed in the United States of America

PINNACLE BOOKS, INC.
1430 Broadway
New York, New York 10018

for:
N. D-H.
who supplies the
finished goods.

MONTANA MELODRAMA

Chapter One

. . . that we know not of? Thus conscience does make cowards of us all. And thus the native hue of resolution. Is sicklied o'er with the pale cast of thought. And enterprises of great pith and moment. With this reward, their currents turn awry. And lose the name of action.

Hamilton Linn bellowed as he completed his bass-voice rendering of the soliloquy from *Hamlet*. For several seconds he stood at the front of the stage in a corner of the Lone Pine Saloon rigid with emotion, hands clasped to his chest and head bowed. His audience, the great majority of whom were spellbound by his histrionics, waited for him to continue—or for the more knowledgeable among their ranks to signal the fact that the costumed actor had finished saying his piece. Finally a frail-looking woman of about sixty who was seated in the front row of the makeshift theater rose to her feet and began to applaud with frenzied excitement.

Meanwhile, out in the chill, moonlit night, a line of six men rode their horses with muffled hooves along the northwest trail that turned into the end of one of the town's two streets. The men were dressed in dark topcoats and wide-brimmed hats that cast thick shadows over their faces. They rode without haste, the skirts of their long coats pulled aside to reveal their hands draped over the butts of holstered revolvers.

In the saloon the actor raised his head and looked at the woman with a wistful expression, as if her noisy enthusiasm had roused him from a reverie that had carried his imagination far away from the confines of this crudely furnished saloon in the Montana lumber town of Ridgeville. Behind him the six other members of the Linn Players sat in a row of chairs, awaiting their turn to perform and surveying the crowded saloon with varying degrees of anxiety. Soon they were beaming as expansively as Linn as other members of the audience rose to join the thin woman in giving the actor a standing ovation.

A group of men at the bar along the rear wall of the saloon turned from watching Linn to retrieve their glasses from the countertop. Several contributed to the noisy enthusiasm for the opening performance of the evening. They returned to their whiskey with a gleeful awareness of the envious glances directed at them by the men in the audience proper.

Diagonally across the street from the noise-filled saloon, the riders reined their mounts to a halt outside the lighted window of the bank and swung out of their saddles. Each man removed the muffles from the hooves of his horse. Then one man gathered the reins of all the animals while the other five drew their revolvers and stepped up to the sidewalk in front of the bank. The door was closed but not locked. One of the gunmen swung it open and stepped across the threshold. As the light of a lamp briefly chased away the shadow of his hat brim one could see that he was wearing a personable smile—unlike the quartet who flanked him, two at either side. Their faces grim, they surveyed the trio of shocked employees, who were working late at the bank—two men and one woman . . . and a pile of bills they were dividing into smaller heaps.

Whether they stood at the bar or were seated on the rows of chairs arranged in lengthening arcs before the platform the men inside the saloon on this unusual evening were mostly of one sort: big, muscular men with weather-beaten features and rough hands who worked in the lumber business. Yet this evening, clothes divided them into two groups—the ones at the bar in workshirts, pants, and boots: the ones sitting down in their Sunday best suits. As the audience started to sit down again a scattering of storekeepers and clerks could also be seen—less well built and paler-skinned men, who were not so obviously uncomfortable as the lumbermen in their suits, collars, and neckties. Some members of this group were unable to conceal the way they coveted the beer and whiskey in the glasses of the men at the bar, who were not accompanied by wives, sweethearts, or mothers dressed in their finest gowns.

Up on the platform, Hamilton Linn enjoyed every moment of the ovation and made no notion to end it until even his most appreciative admirer began to flag. Then at last he held up both hands to request silence.

3

"Good people of this fine town of Ridgeville," he boomed, "from the bottom of my heart I thank you. I and my company of players have appeared on the hallowed boards of some of the greatest theatrical stages of the country. But I cannot recall an occasion when we were received with such warmth and regard. We feel very humble."

He paused, as if expecting a response. When it did not come, he continued, a little reluctantly perhaps, since what he was saying meant he had to surrender the center stage. "And now, good ladies and gentlemen, as a further prelude . . . to the week of full-length dramas we intend to perform before you in the meeting hall, may I present Miss Elizabeth Miles, who will regale you, in her inimitable style, with the balcony speech from the Bard's *Romeo and Juliet*. Miss Miles."

The two kerosene lamps that hung immediately above the front of the platform were shaded by a beam so that only a fringe of their light reached the row of seated performers at the rear. Thus, the actress could not be seen clearly until she rose and advanced out of the shadows. As she emerged into view, the smattering of polite applause that had greeted her introduction abruptly swelled, whistles and raucous shouts supplementing the hand-clapping.

The man who held the horses outside the bank wrenched his head around to stare across the street at the sudden burst of noise from the saloon. Then he returned his attention to the open doorway of the bank.

"Anyone makes a sound, this'll top it," the smiling man said evenly, waving his Frontier Colt.

4

"And ain't one of you people'll be around to see if you saved the money from us."

"On account of you'll all be dead!" the youngest of the grim-faced gunmen snarled softly.

"We ain't so stupid as we seem to be, kid," growled one of the late-night workers, who happened to be wearing a lawman's badge on his vest. "We know what your boss means."

"But do you men know what you're getting into?" asked the woman, a thin, middle-aged creature in spectacles.

"Yes, ma'am," the smiling man answered as two others holstered their revolvers and took large sacks from their coat pockets. "We're gettin' into the rich life."

Several women in the audience in the Lone Pine Saloon frowned at their menfolk. They knew that the men were applauding the actress for the wrong reason. Because Elizabeth Miles was a tall blond in her mid-twenties with an aristocratic beauty and a fine figure. In her striking green dress, which revealed the upper swells of her powdered breasts and tightly hugged and supported the lower halves, it was inevitable that every red-blooded man in the saloon—where culture was a word few knew the meaning of—should be more interested in the young woman's natural endowments than in the lines she now started to deliver.

Not least of her admirers was a stranger in town who was among those grouped at the bar.

At a lean six feet three inches tall and weighing in the region of two hundred pounds, he might well have been taken for a logger at first glance, though he was not so employed. He had features that would by some be regarded as handsome and by others as ugly—piercing light blue eyes under hooded lids, a hawklike nose, and a narrow mouth that had a somewhat cruel set to it. His skin, stretched taut across his brow and between his high cheekbones and firm jawline, was of a darker hue than any other man's in the saloon—and was inscribed with more and deeper lines than was usual for somebody not yet forty years of age.

This face was framed by jet-black hair that was long enough to brush his shoulders and veil the nape of his neck. Though he had recently shaved, an arc of bristles as black as his hair curved away from his flared nostrils and down at either side of his mouth as if to emphasize the fact that a large proportion of Latin blood flowed in his veins.

His garb was entirely of the American West, from the gray Stetson to the spurless riding boots. He wore a dark-hued shirt and no kerchief, so that a row of dull-colored beads could be seen at the base of his throat where the top button of his shirt was unfastened. Despite these beads, he did not seem to be the kind of man who favored ornamentation for its own sake. And certainly the revolver, which jutted from the tied-down holster on the right side of his plain gunbelt, was a standard Frontier Colt with no fancy scrollwork on the butt, cylinder, or barrel.

The fact that he was the only man in the saloon wearing a gun set him apart from the others. His stance and the way he surveyed his surroundings through permanently narrowed lids were more subtle indications that he was not a part of the lumbermen, clerks, and storekeepers, all of whom were watching without listening to the beautiful young actress up on the brightly lit area of the platform.

The stranger's name was Edge.

Across the street from the saloon, a man emerged from the bank, gun still drawn. He gave the one holding the horses a thumbs-up sign that all was well inside. The lookout on the street could not control a giggle of relief.

In the bank, the lawman muttered: "The Campbells oughta know better than to allow this."

"Who the hell are the Campbells?" a gunman countered.

"We came here for money, not friggin' conversation!" another rasped uneasily.

Inside the saloon Edge watched the show, his face revealing nothing of what he thought of it. There were many men like Edge in the territory west of the Mississippi, south of Canada, and north of Mexico. Men who invariably stood out in a crowd because it was not in their natures to be as one with others. Drifting loners who rode wherever the trail led and were never totally at ease, even out under the big sky, but who were most suspicious of their surroundings when the trail brought them into a community where the local citizens viewed them as unwelcome intruders who were not to be trusted. A threat, not by their deeds but simply by their presence, to their conventional and well-ordered lives.

So it was that intruders like Edge had been taught by the experiences of many dangerous years to trust nothing and nobody. Taught to be on their guard against losing their lives—not simply their life-styles. Indeed, to lose the latter might seem to them to be worse than dying.

7

Elizabeth Miles completed her contribution to the evening's entertainment and accepted the applause with smiling gratitude—aware though she was that the more raucous elements were expressing their appreciation of her appearance rather than her performance. She was obviously accustomed to being employed by Hamilton Linn to inject the spice of sex into highbrow drama on those occasions when the attention of the audience was likely to wander.

"Wow, that is some woman," growled a barrel-chested man at the bar as Linn rose and advanced to the front of the stage. The actress backed to her seat with just the trace of a scowl at the costumed man for stealing the limelight too soon. "Be real happy to give her a part in the kinda long-runnin' play I got in mind."

A short and skinny bartender with red hair vented a short laugh and retorted: "With a woman like that, Chapman, I reckon you wouldn't be able to perform more than one act before it was curtains for you! What do you say, stranger?"

Edge pushed his empty glass across the countertop and replied evenly: "Another beer is all, feller."

"Sure thing."

Chapman muttered, "Wish *she* was," and swallowed what was left of the liquor in his shot glass as the bartender began to draw Edge's beer and Hamilton Linn started to intone: "On behalf of Miss Miles, I thank . . ."

All the gunmen were out of the bank now and in the process of mounting their horses—four with guns still drawn while two toted bulky sacks. None of them spoke until the closed door of the bank was wrenched open and the lawman lunged over the threshold, a double-barrel shotgun thrust out in front of him.

"Watch it, you guys!"

"I'll teach the friggin' Campbells!"

The lawman squeezed the two triggers of the shotgun as a man behind him shrieked, "It's not loaded, Bart!"

Four of the men already astride their horses fired shots to cover those who were not yet mounted. And the lawman staggered and sprawled across the sidewalk, bloodstains blossoming around two holes in his chest.

The other two shots found a different target—the dread-filled face of the man who had appeared in the doorway to warn the lawman that the shotgun was empty. The impact of the bullets slammed his head against the doorframe, then his legs bent and he pitched forward, slumping over the corpse of the lawman.

The bespectacled woman was screaming her terror and grief by then. The two emotions contorted her face as she stumbled out of the bank and made to crouch beside the stricken men. But she was forced upright and then sent sprawling backward across the threshold as four bullets drilled into her chest and head . . . to curtail her screaming.

Guns were holstered as smoke drifted. The riders turned their horses and then kicked them into a headlong gallop back along the street. Oozing blood stained clothing or trickled across the flesh of faces set in agonized death masks.

In the saloon, the man on the platform demanded, "What on earth was that?"

Only the first word was clearly audible above the hoofbeats as the riders raced their mounts away from the area of the saloon. And only few heard the man complete the query through the din that erupted inside the Lone Pine. The din of raised voices, heavy footfalls hitting the floor, and chairs toppling over. The audience was lost to the Linn Players, as they hurried to witness the real-life drama that was being enacted out on the street.

The bartender was in the thick of the mass exodus, leaving Edge's beer mug only half-filled under the tap. So Edge had to lean across the countertop to finish the chore for himself. He put some coins on the bar to pay for the drink and carried it through the almost empty saloon toward the batwing doors that were still flapping.

"Sir?" Linn called from the platform where he stood with arms outstretched, to keep the two women and four men of his theatrical company from following the local citizens.

"Yeah, feller?"

"In some of the Kansas cattle towns we have played, it was quite common for the more youthful drovers to explode guns on the street as a means of releasing their exuberance?"

"Didn't sound to me like everybody was having fun out there," Edge replied and pushed out through the door.

Linn started to tell his company, "We should not concern ourselves in business which is none of . . ."

The half-breed heard no more as he moved away from the front of the saloon to head for the bank.

10

The two-street town of Ridgeville was situated on the Little Creek tributary of the Yellowstone River in the eastern foothills of the Beartooth Mountains, just north of the Wyoming line. The streets were laid out in the form of a cross on a flat area of land in a curve of the sixty-foot-wide creek. As a result, the northeast end of one street and the southeast of the other were blocked by the fast-flowing water of the creek.

The Lone Pine Saloon was on the northwest corner of the streets' intersection, and as Edge sipped his beer he saw it was to the northwest that the riders had galloped. Their forms were already lost in the timber that crowded close to town on that side. He also saw that their hurried departure had started diagonally across the street from the saloon, in front of the Timberline Bank and Trust Company, where the former audience in the Lone Pine had now gathered. A grim quiet reigned in the vicinity of the recent tragedy.

As Edge reached the rear of the crowd one of the men who was not uncomfortable in a suit emerged from the lighted doorway of the bank and asked tensely, "What's the verdict, Doc?"

A man in shirt-sleeves who had not been in the saloon rose from where he had been squatting on the sidewalk to reply: "All dead, Mr. Sheldon."

"What did they get, Sheldon?" a gruff-voiced man demanded from the shocked crowd.

"Company shipment is all gone and the safe is cleaned out."

"Everything?" a woman called shrilly. "They've taken every last cent?"

"Looks like, Mrs. Reese."

"Then I'm ruined!"

11

"You ain't the only one, lady!"

"What'll we do?"

"This is terrible, terrible!"

"Will none of you people spare a thought for the Trasks and Mr. Bolt?"

"Dammit, their troubles are over! How are we supposed to get by with just the loose change we got in our pockets?"

The sallow-faced, sandy-haired man named Sheldon held up his hands to quiet the chorus of voices. Then he said: "I intend to leave for Casper right now. To bring money to replace that which has been stolen. And men to hunt down the thieves. So don't any of you people do anything foolish now. Like going after them yourselves."

"It was the friggin' Campbells, I bet! Bart Bolt should've hung them when he had the chance!"

Voices were raised to agree and disagree with this. And Sheldon shouted for attention again. Edge was on his way back to the saloon by then, having sipped his way through half the beer while he bleakly surveyed the bullet-riddled corpses of the town sheriff and the banker and his wife.

Sheldon yelled: "So you company men can be certain you'll get paid within the week! And I feel sure the businessmen of this town will extend credit for that period wherever it is necessary!"

Another chorus of voices expressed a restrained satisafction and the crowd began to disperse.

The Linn Players had advanced to the front of the Lone Pine but seemed reluctant to go closer to the scene of the triple shooting. They all looked as terrified as most of the Ridgeville citizens sounded.

"Did we hear correctly, sir?" Linn asked

huskily. "The bank has been robbed of every cent?"

Edge drained his glass and thrust it toward the youngest male member of the company, an effeminate boy of about eighteen who took the glass automatically and was surprised to find himself holding it. "Be obliged if you'd return this when you go back inside. Yeah, feller. Opinion seems to be that a bunch called the Campbells got away with everything in the bank. Killed three people in the process."

"Oh, my God!" Linn gasped. "What are we going to do? The entire receipts after expenses from a four month sell-out tour."

"Aw, shit!" the beautiful Elizabeth Miles rasped, speaking her thought aloud. Then, more forcefully: "Isn't anybody going to go after the thieves?" Her flashing green eyes shifted from the dispersing crowd on the street to her frowning fellow players and then settled on Edge.

The half-breed shook his head as he patted his hip pocket. "I take personal care of what's mine, lady."

"And so long as you're all right, it doesn't matter about anybody else?" She sneered.

"Why should it?"

"No reason, mister. Except that you look like the kind of man who makes a living out of other people's troubles."

Edge nodded. "Sometimes I do, lady."

"But who around this town can afford to pay you now?"

"Nobody, I guess. But I ain't looking for work anyway." As he swung away from the anxious

13

frown of Linn and the scowl of Elizabeth Miles, he patted his hip pocket again. "I already told you, lady. The Campbells didn't leave me in the soup."

Chapter Two

BECAUSE Ridgeville was not on a major trail to anywhere and boasted of nothing to attract tourists, the town had no hotel. There was a boardinghouse just across from the Lone Pine Saloon; it was run by a frail old spinster who had been so appreciative of Hamilton Linn's performance. Normally it catered to the needs of itinerant loggers; and from its run-down appearance these were few and far between.

Edge had been told to try his luck at Miss Emma's place by the redheaded bartender when he first reached Ridgeville at midday. But the little old lady had claimed that all her rooms were taken by the Linn Players. He did not believe this because the two-story house was too big and rambling to be fully occupied by the theatrical company. And his impression that she was lying was strengthened by her frosty attitude toward him: making it plain that she did not approve of the way he looked.

Nevertheless Miss Emma did tell him that John James down at the livery sometimes allowed strangers to sleep in his stalls. And she added

15

with a sniff that the qualifications for this privilege seemed to be a capacity to match drink for drink with John James and a ready ear for his endless stories that interested nobody but himself.

So it was to the JJ Livery Stables that Edge went now, moving at a slow and easy gait along the southeastern stretch of Pine Street. All the way down to where it ended at the bank of the creek, the sheer, curved face of the sixty-foot-high Indian Bluff looming across the other side.

He walked between the darkened and shuttered façades of business premises, for Pine was the commercial street of Ridgeville. The second street, which was called Douglas, was lined on both sides with houses, a few of which were owned by the town's businessmen but most by the lumber company, which rented them to its employees.

A gleam of light showed through a crack in the big double doors of the livery. Edge assumed this meant that the owner of the place was not yet bedded down. Before he opened one of the doors, the half-breed struck a match on the butt of his Colt and lit the cigarette he had rolled while walking down the street.

"If I'd known them theatricals was gonna play-act somethin' excitin' with shootin' and stuff like they done, I mighta come see it," John James growled as Edge stood on the threshold, peering out at the street where a man was hurrying toward him. He recognized him as the company man, Sheldon, now wearing a topcoat and hat.

The livery was a large establishment with a dozen stalls along each wall and a living area at the rear. It was as clean as a working stable ever could be. There were just two empty stalls, which was a measure of JJ's success at his business. Halfway down the central aisle a ladder led up to the trapdoor that opened into the hayloft. Edge waited until he had walked past this before he said: "The shooting was for real, JJ. Bunch of men just robbed the bank. Killed the banker and his wife and your local lawman."

James was about fifty. Short and overweight, he sported a potbelly and a pair of breasts that resembled those of a girl on the verge of puberty. If he had bought any new clothes since his body and limbs had begun to run to fat, Edge had not seen him in them. The stained pants and undershirt he wore were contoured to his every fleshy bulge. He was bald except for a ring of gray hair that reached from ear to ear around the back of his head. There was more gray hair sprouting along his top lip in a bushy mustache. His face was round and he had bulbous cheeks that crowded his small, dark eyes.

The unhealthy ruddiness of his complexion, the glaze in his eyes, and the sloppiness of his garb marked him as a drunk. But the livery business paid him enough so that he could afford the liquor. And he always kept his wits sufficiently about him to do a good job of tending to horse-flesh—on the premise that if he was ever too drunk to do his chores, he would lose out on the business he needed to buy more liquor.

"Bart Bolt and Joe and Amy Trask are dead?" He was instantly as sober as he probably ever got. "Sonofabitch! Good old Bart was in here havin' a snort . . . couldn't have been more than ten minutes before the shootin'. Sonofabitch!"

"It sure is that right enough, JJ," Sheldon growled as he entered the livery. "Money isn't important, though I suppose the company won't view it that way when they have to come up with more to meet the payroll."

He entered one of the stalls close to the front of the stable without pausing in his bitter-toned talk. "It's terrible about the sheriff and Mr. and Mrs. Trask being gunned down that way. But rest assured, JJ. The Campbell gang will not get away with this. The company has the funds and connections to locate and hire the best men available to hunt down and bring the culprits to justice."

The living quarters were not partitioned off from the rest of the stable. They occupied a twenty-foot by twenty-foot area which was crowded with a narrow bed, a table and two chairs, a closet, and a cooking range. A fire was burning in the range.

Edge did not become aware of just how chilly the night air had been until he felt the warmth from the glowing grate of the range. He sat down in the chair across the table from the grim-faced liveryman and listened to Sheldon. Edge smoked and JJ started to drink again. With a single shot of rye whiskey he seemed to get drunk in as short a time as he had appeared to sober up a few moments before.

A pot of coffee was bubbling on the range; its aroma went some way to negate the smell of horses and human body odor that otherwise pervaded the atmosphere. As JJ poured himself another drink and Sheldon urged his horse from its stall, Edge rose from the table and went to the range. He took a tin mug down from a nearby shelf and filled it with coffee.

"Good night to you, gentlemen," the lumber company man called as he led his mount out of the stable. "They'll pay for what they did. By God, how they'll pay!"

If JJ heard what Sheldon promised as the door closed behind him, he was not impressed by it. He simply threw his new drink down his throat and poured another.

Edge sipped the strong coffee and remained standing at the range. Sensing that his host was getting ready to talk, and prepared, for a while, to be the passive listener that Miss Emma had said was one of the requirements for being allowed to bed down at the livery. He had spent much of the afternoon in the same way, while the liveryman attended to his chores and related the story of his life.

JJ offered Edge a drink, but took no offense when it was declined. Neither had the older man been miffed when the half-breed drifted off to sleep on his bedroll in a stall, lulled by JJ's voice and the gurgling sounds of the fast-flowing Little Creek. For when the liveryman nudged Edge awake three hours later, it was to invite him to share a meal of well-cooked pork and beans.

"Was gonna be payday for the company men tomorrow. And for folks like me that do business with company men. Time for us to collect on all the credit we been givin'. The trail from Casper got washed out for a while and ain't no company man been paid for more than a month." When JJ started to talk, he peered down the central aisle of the stable. Now he allowed his head to drop for-

19

ward so he was gazing into the shot glass he gripped in his big hands. "When good old Bart left here he said he was gonna go by the bank and see if the Trasks needed a hand. To divide the money from the big boxes into the little packets that each man was supposed to get this mornin'. It is after midnight now, ain't it, mister?"

One of the big doors at the front of the livery opened again and Hamilton Linn entered. He was no longer in his Shakespearian costume and he looked shorter and thinner in a cream-colored duster coat and a black derby. Older, too. He was probably on the brink of sixty. Five and a half feet tall and several pounds underweight.

Edge had not been aware that the man was wearing theatrical makeup in the saloon. Without it, he was seen to have a pale and waxy complexion with sunken eyes and hollow cheeks, a thin and crooked nose, a sour-looking mouth, and a weak jaw.

"Good old Bart was about the only friend I had, I reckon," JJ muttered.

"What the sheriff was, sir, was too old for his job," Hamilton Linn boomed out, in a bass voice that was as strong offstage as on.

The liveryman wrenched his head up to glare with drunken resentment at the newcomer and demanded: "Who the frig asked you to butt in?"

Linn was momentarily taken aback by the degree of venom in JJ's voice. But then he nodded sagely when he saw the man at the table pour another drink from the now just quarter-full bottle. "I came here to speak with you, Mr. Edge," he said after dismissing JJ with a grimace of disgust. "To request your assistance."

20

"Helping other people is what other people do, feller," the half-breed answered.

"I'll friggin' help you, mister!" JJ snarled, springing up from the table, glass in one hand and bottle in the other. "Comin' in here runnin' off at the mouth about good old Bart. I'll help you outta my place! With the friggin' toe of my friggin' boot! If you don't turn right around and leave under your own friggin' steam!"

Linn spared another grimacing glance for JJ. He saw that the man was swaying on his splayed legs and could barely keep his slack mouth closed after throwing whiskey into it, so that most of the liquor ran down his jaw. Then the actor returned his level gaze to the impassive face of Edge and promised: "It will be to your financial advantage if you hear me out and agree to the proposition I put to you, sir."

JJ hurled the empty glass against a wall but continued to grip the uncapped bottle by the neck. "You hear me, mister!" he snarled. "You and your bunch is stayin' at the old crone's place! And takin' care of your nags in her stable! So you got no business to do in my livery! And where you're standing right now is in my livin' quarters! Where no one comes unless I friggin' invite them! And I ain't even invitin' you to leave, mister! I'm friggin' tellin' you!"

He came out from behind the table to get close to the actor. Linn stood his ground and spread a sneer of contempt across his thin face, unafraid of the much heavier man who was consumed by drunken rage and apparently lacking in any kind of coordination between his mind and muscles.

"You have liquor where your mind should be,

21

sir!" Linn boomed. "Why do you not return to your chair and sit down before you fall down?"

JJ reacted to this the same way he had reacted when Edge told him three people had died from the shooting down the street. It was as if he had not taken a drink in weeks—but on this occasion his anger was far greater and had a ready target to give it outlet.

He made as if to swing around and go back to the table—to do as the actor had tauntingly suggested. But in reality the move was made for the sake of lengthening the arc of the bottle, now suddenly become a club. His hand was fisted around its neck and rose high as he drew back his arm.

Hamilton Linn spotted the movement as an attack and was suddenly afraid. Not of being hurt, but of what he was certain he had to do to keep from having the bottle smashed against the side of his head. He felt this as his left hand delved into the pocket of his duster. Edge heard the telltale click of a gun hammer being cocked an instant before Linn yelled: "Don't be a fool!"

The half-breed rasped a curse through clenched teeth as he dropped his mug of coffee and lunged forward in a partial crouch. His right shoulder canted to thud against the upper left arm of Hamilton Linn; his left hand clawed to catch hold of JJ's swinging bottle.

The actor went into a sideways sprawl with a cry of alarm that sounded in unison with the crack of a gunshot. And Edge moved instinctively to get clear of the small-caliber bullet that tore out of Linn's coat pocket. He smelled the scorch of the bullet-holed coat fabric.

The liveryman turned to track the falling Linn

22

with glowering eyes and in his rage was not even aware that Edge had sent the actor crashing to the floor. Then JJ gave vocal vent to an even greater degree of fury, as the bottle made shattering impact with an unseen target just short of Hamilton Linn.

Edge felt a bolt of agony as the bottle thudded against his left temple. He glimpsed through a spray of liquor and broken glass the shocked face of the man he had knocked to the floor. Heard JJ curtail his shriek of high anger. Smelt the spilled whiskey. Wondered if he was seeing the actor with both eyes or if one was blinded by shards of bottle glass imbedded in it. Sensed he was an instant away from slumping into unconsciousness—that his powerful lunge toward Linn was about to end as a limp-limbed collapse.

"You've killed him!" the actor boomed.

Pitching facedown into a bottomless black hole, the half-breed heard the voice of JJ responding to Linn but was unable to discern what the liveryman was saying.

Then a woman spoke, very clearly. She said: "Shit, it makes me feel sick just to look at it."

And Edge was surprised to hear his own voice say—when he was certain he had only thought— "You shouldn't speak ill of the dead, lady."

Chapter Three

ELIZABETH Miles vented her own surprise in a gasp and Edge had a fleeting impression of her flinching away from him as he cracked open his eyes. Fleeting because the dazzlingly bright light that lanced against his eyes sparked an explosion of intense pain under his skull—which was only marginally eased when he dropped his hooded lids.

"Go ahead and cry out, Mr. Edge," the actress urged in a hard and biting tone. "It isn't possible for me to think any the less of you. And there's no one else to hear you."

For what seemed a very long time, the half-breed hated her. Not for what she had said. His teeth were gritted and his lips curled back in an ugly snarl to prevent a scream of pain from bursting out of his throat. And the look on his face was just one result of how his body was reacting to the searing agony in his head—his muscles drawing the skin taut between every bone of his frame. He hated her simply because of the sound of her voice—each syllable seeming to compound the thudding pain.

24

But it was simply his punished brain playing tricks with time. The agony remained at a high peak of intensity for just a few seconds. And when he cautiously cracked open his eyelids he quickly saw he had been tricked once before—that the period between hearing the mumbling words of JJ and the crystal-clear voice of Elizabeth Miles had been far longer than he had at first thought. For the dazzling brilliance which had so unexpectedly assaulted his eyes was not from a kerosene lamp. It was simply sunlight shafting down on to him through a window.

"To me, you're a pain in the ass anyway. But don't take that personally. I regard all men the same way."

"You've got a bad mouth, Miss Miles," he rasped through the gritted teeth. "But you should know that each time you open it, it ain't my feelings you're hurting."

"If you'll just hold still, I can do what's necessary without talking, Edge. Or you can give my day a really fine start by telling me to get the hell out of here. That you'd prefer somebody else to act as your nurse."

Edge saw they were in the JJ Livery Stables without needing to raise his head. In the stall by the south window that John James had allocated to him. Stretched out on his bedroll in the straw-layered floor of the stall. Fully dressed except for his hat and his boots. The woman was kneeling beside him, dressed in tight-fitting blue denim pants and an open-necked check shirt: an outfit that in its own way displayed the feminine curves of her slender body and limbs as alluringly as the gown she had worn the last time he'd seen her.

25

There was no makeup on her face this morning and she did not look so classically beautiful. Looked better for it, he thought. Younger and fresher. Maybe twenty-two or three, with a flawless complexion in the bright sunlight. Green eyes and full, pouting lips. Her blond hair hung down below her shoulders at the front and back, in natural waves that were a little unruly. So she was, offstage, a lot closer to Shakespeare's conception of the teenage Juliet: but then the playwright had never had to consider that his lines would not be sufficient in themselves to hold the undivided attention of a saloon filled with tough Montana lumbermen.

Edge was not familiar enough with the classic love story to know if Juliet was ever called upon to scowl the way Elizabeth Miles did as she waited for a response from him.

"What's needed, lady?" He turned his head on the blanket pillow and limited his reaction to the fresh pain this caused to a grimace. "But if just looking at me makes folks want to throw up, I'd just as soon take care of it myself."

There was a bowl of water on the straw to one side of her, hot enough to give off a steamy medicinal smell. Close by was a wad of rag caked with crusted blood. A pile of clean white rags.

"I was talking to the horse in the next stall, Edge. About the mess that bottle made of the side of your head. Doc Hunter said the old dressing had to be taken off and the wound cleaned up. And, oh yeah, he said that if you woke up, I was to ask if you're seeing clearly. And if you can recall what happened to you."

"Clear, but not plain," he told her. And experimented with a grin, trying to inject some warmth into the glittering slits of his eyes. He was anxious to feel better and stronger and knew this would happen faster if he did not have to attend to his own needs.

"I know I'm attractive to men, mister," Elizabeth Miles growled. "Flattery from them doesn't make me go weak at the knees or any of that shit."

Edge sighed. "It ain't just my knees that are weak, lady. Be obliged if you'd do what you were told. Or get somebody else to fix me up."

She grunted her satisfaction and expressed the trace of what might have been a smile. She soaked a piece of clean rag in the hot water as she said, "Hold still, this is going to hurt."

"Me more than you, lady."

She pressed the dripping rag to his temple and he caught his breath as the heat and medication of the water seared the lacerated skin. He snapped his hooded lids closed, but tears squeezed out and crawled across his deeply lined flesh. Then the initial onslaught of this new brand of pain diminished and the warmth and medication in the water began to have a soothing effect.

He became aware of the woman's gentleness as she bathed his wound, and when he opened his eyes he saw with a stab of mild disappointment that the scowl of dislike was still firmly fixed upon her face. "Did the liveryman and your boss kill each other?" he asked as she dispensed with the stained rag and soaked a fresh one.

"So you're not seeing double and your memory

is all right. I'll be able to tell Doc Hunter what he wanted to know."

"But me nothing?"

"Hamilton Linn isn't my boss, Edge. He's just one of the company of players who happens to own the wagon we travel in. No, they didn't harm each other. Turned to jelly when they thought you were dead. Then shook worse than ever when they saw you were still alive. Scared you'll blame them for what happened to you."

"Be nursing a sore head for a while, I guess. But it was nobody's fault but my own."

She again started to dab gently at the area of broken skin on his temple. "The longer Ham Linn doesn't know that the better, as far as I'm concerned. Worth the female lead in a big-city run to know that pompous old fool is quaking in his drawers."

She set aside the wet rag and began to dry off the excess moisture, then dumped all the rags—dirty and clean—into the bowl and lifted this as she rose to her feet. "The doc got all the glass splinters out of you last night. Told me that if there was no sign of infection, it'll be best to leave off a dressing. Heal up better if the air gets to it."

Sprawled flat on his back, looking up the lengths of her denim-contoured legs and across the flatness of her belly to the mounds of her breasts hugged by the shirt, Edge experienced a surge of sexual desire that briefly transcended the thudding ache inside his skull. It was immediately dulled when he became certain that this was what she expected—that she was deliberately flaunting her body to arouse him sexually—for the sheer pleasure it gave her to be wanted and unattainable. "Obliged for your help, lady," he said. "I owe you."

"Not a thing, mister. Me and the rest of the company were waiting outside when we heard the shot. Were still in here when the doc was fetched. It just happened I was closest when he was through patching you up and he asked me to keep an eye on you."

"And I had the impression you're the kind of woman who always says no."

She shrugged. "It had more appeal than spending the night with Linn and the others—listening to them crying about losing our money and not doing a damn thing to get it back."

"JJ?"

"That drunken sonofabitch rode off into the woods with a gun and a couple of bottles of booze. Yelling about how he plans to make the bank raiders pay for killing the only friend he had left. Anything you want before I go?"

He raised a hand to touch his brow. "My skull feels twice the size it should be, lady. So if you could give me a little head . . ."

She vented a short sigh of disgust and swung away from him, her rump swaying inside the tight grip of her pants as she went out of the stall.

The grin Edge had started to spread across his face died when he closed his eyes and endured in gritted-toothed silence the regular pounding in his head that matched the cadence of her strides down the central aisle of the livery.

"A stable is the ideal place for you, mister!" she yelled. "Since you appear to have the morals of a stallion at stud!"

He could not prevent a wince when she slammed one of the big doors behind her. Then he rasped sourly: "With no chance of getting a bit on the side."

Chapter Four

RIDGEVILLE was quite literally a quiet town. Or so Edge discovered as he lay in the stall for about thirty minutes waiting for the ache in his head to ease and gradually became aware of the community coming to what could only be called lethargic life.

First he smelled wood smoke, then the aromas of coffee and food. Next came the sounds of opening doors and windows. Later footfalls and the thud of hooves and the rattle of rigs on the move. Finally an occasional call of greeting followed by intermittent snatches of conversation which reached him as no more than a multi-toned murmuring.

He was up and out of the stall by then. Initially he felt dazed and in danger of suffering from the double vision the local doctor had considered a possible result of the blow. But this soon cleared and he felt as hungry as if the smell of cooking breakfasts had started rumbling sounds in his stomach. The fire in the range was still burning and in no more than a few minutes after pulling on his boots, he had water heating for a shave and for coffee and some bacon and beans frying in a skillet.

He shaved before he ate, sitting at the table and removing the straight razor from a pouch that hung from the beaded thong around his neck. That he could find no mirror in the livery was no obstacle to this procedure, for there were few mornings when he did not have to shave blind. Then he had breakfast and smoked a cigarette with a second mug of coffee while he absently fingered the area of broken skin on his temple.

Outside, the creek gurgled and the town's daily business got under way with a minimum of noise in the commercial premises of Pine Street. Just the horses belonging to Sheldon and John James were gone from the livery, and nobody entered to take out any of the other animals standing contentedly in their warm, sun-bright stalls.

Edge cleaned up after the morning shaving and breakfast ritual and saddled his black mare. She was a big, strong animal, clear-eyed and intelligent, who had carried him a lot of miles to reach this timber town in the mountains. And the western saddle he cinched to her was hung with all the accoutrements a man on a long ride through largely uninhabited country might require. What essentials were not hung from the saddle or packed in the two bags were wrapped in or attached to the bedroll which he furled and fixed on behind the saddle. When he'd first gotten up, he'd grimaced while he waited for the fuzziness to leave him. But now Edge's lean and dark-hued face was set in an expression of total impassiveness which was a true indication of his state of mind.

Abruptly his ice-blue eyes looked colder than the depths of winter. This occurred as he delved a hand into a pocket of his pants and failed to find the loose change that should have been there. Then, when he moved his hand to dip into his hip pocket, his thin lips drew back to display his teeth in a snarl, an expression that revealed the capacity for cruelty which the more discerning were able to see lurking just beneath the invariably calm exterior of this man.

By the time he led the mare down the central aisle of the livery and out to Pine Street, however, his features were back to their implacable set. There was no visible clue to the casual observer, as he easily swung up astride the saddle and heeled the horse forward, to how he felt about being robbed.

The sidewalks along this stretch of street were sparsely peopled with women shoppers, some of whom acknowledged him. Others pointedly ignored him, as they had when he rode into Ridgeville yesterday. While some members of the local populace were naturally friendly, others plainly disapproved of the appearance of a lone stranger with a Colt in a tied-down holster, a Winchester jutting from a forward-hung boot, and eyes as cold as high mountain ice—eyes that surveyed their surroundings with a suspicion honed sharp by long experience. Edge touched the brim of his hat with a forefinger in response to those who nodded, smiled, or spoke a soft-voiced greeting to him. He ignored the reproachful gazes and reproving exchanges. Slowly he had rode past the people.

The only men he saw were old-timers and those who worked at supplying goods and services to the town. The majority of the male population of Ridgeville was out working at the several company camps in the timberland that surrounded the town or at the sawmill a couple of miles to the south. From this direction he heard the muted thud of a steam engine at work. He rode to the center of the intersection, halted the mare, and tugged on the reins to turn the animal toward the façade of Miss Emma's boardinghouse on the corner of Pine and Douglas streets.

The people who were still watching him—either with idle curiosity or surreptitious hostility—were suddenly afraid. For they saw him slowly draw the Colt from the holster, thumb back the hammer, and aim the gun.

Then squeeze the trigger.

The crack of the bullet blasting from the muzzle sounded in unison with the clang of a bell clapper as the shell scored a hit in the ornamental brass bell that hung beside the front door of the boardinghouse.

The thud of the ricocheting bullet could not be heard. It was masked by shouts of alarm, the slap of running footfalls, and the wrenching open of doors and windows. Then there was a sudden silence, disturbed only by the sounds of the creek and the more distant noise of the steam engine at the sawmill, as the townsfolk who had reached a position to see the cause of the gunshot gazed uncomprehendingly at the mounted man on the center of the intersection. He was nonchalantly ejecting the spent shellcase from a smoking chamber of his Colt and sliding a fresh round into the revolver.

Many of the occupants of the boardinghouse also watched the man with amazement. Miss Emma was the first one to show herself, thudding open an upper-story window with violent force and leaning out to glare at Edge. A scarf was tied about her gray hair and her red-cheeked face was smudged from a cleaning chore. "Just what do you think you are doing, you crazy man?" she demanded.

The half-breed slid the reloaded Colt back into the holster and cracked his hooded eyes to the narrowest slits as he looked up at the irate old lady and the brilliantly blue morning sky above the roof of her house. He touched the brim of his hat. "May just be one of your boarders I need to talk to, Miss Emma. On the other hand, could be the whole town needs to hear what I have to say."

"Mr. Edge! You want to come by the office and let me take a look at you?"

The half-breed glanced up and saw the tall, thin, distinguished-looking Doc Hunter standing in front of a building two doors down from the bank that had been robbed. There was an anxious frown on his age-lined face. "Got an ache in my head is all, feller. What concerns me more is what I ain't got in my hip pocket anymore."

He returned his glinting-eyed gaze to the porch of the boardinghouse as the door opened and Elizabeth Miles stepped angrily over the threshold.

"Just what is that supposed to mean mister?" she snarled.

"Near a thousand dollars is what ain't there, lady."

The relevation triggered a buzz of talk among the bystanders. The half-breed did not allow his attention to shift from the doorway of the boardinghouse. Elizabeth Miles seemed to be both shocked and insulted. But Edge reminded himself that she was a professional actress.

"Are you implying that . . ." she began heatedly as she advanced to the front of the porch. She rested her fists on her hips and seemed set to spit at him. Then her voice rose to a shriller tone. "Yes, you sure as hell are! You really do disgust me, you know that, Edge? After last night's bank raid, most people in this town are flat broke. But just because we're barnstormers, the first people you think to accuse of robbing you are me and Linn and the others!" Her green eyes directed a glare of deep-seated hatred toward Edge that seemed to have a palpable force.

Miss Emma shrieked shrilly, "Don't you go spreadin' vile rumors about the folks hereabouts, young woman! Ridgeville people are decent and honest!"

"Damn right!" the redheaded bartender yelled over the tops of the batwing doors. "Maybe the Campbells have took most of the cash money we had! But look around you! It's business as usual! Everybody trustin' everybody else to pay for what they're buyin' when we're back on our feet!"

"Just because I said we didn't take his money, I don't mean to—" the actress began, contrition visible and audible through the anger she still felt toward Edge.

"You ain't thinkin' straight, mister!" Miss Emma

interrupted from the window. "Either on account of that knock on your head or because you're just plain dumb!"

"Take care, Miss Emma!" the bartender warned anxiously.

"Shoot to that, Moss Tracy!" the old lady countered without shifting her beady-eyed gaze from the impassive face of Edge. "He don't frighten me! Hear this, mister, there's just the one exception among the folks I was speakin' of! And if you'd thought about it before ridin' down here to shoot up the town, you'd have figured it out for yourself! Just two people ain't doin' what's usual for them on a weekday mornin'!

"One's Bill Sheldon who's lit out for Casper to get replacement money to pay the company men! And the other's that no good drunken John James who's just lit out! For no good reason anyone knew about until you started accusin' decent folks of robbin' you!"

As she concluded her shrill-voiced piece of logic, then slammed the window closed, another buzz of excited talk reached Edge. But after a few moments it quieted and Ridgeville continued on about its business, everyone apparently convinced that Miss Emma had hit upon the solution to the mystery.

Edge remained open-minded as he watched Elizabeth Miles come down the two steps from the porch and stride toward him. She came to a halt immediately in front of the horse, her legs slightly splayed and her fists back on her hips. There was a fire of aggression in her green eyes and patches of color in her cheeks. But she kept her voice to a low hiss.

37

"I don't know who stole your lousy money, Edge. And, quite frankly, I don't give a shit! Unless I'm maybe a little pleased about it. What with you being so high and mighty about looking after what is yours after the bank raid. But you take heed of this, mister. It wasn't me. It was me went to bring Doc Hunter. And while I was bringing him, a whole lot of people came to the stable to find out what the shooting was about. And I didn't sit up mopping your fevered brow all night. Most of the time I was sleeping. And when I'm asleep, a whole army could march by me and I wouldn't know it."

Edge nodded. "Obliged."

"Does that mean you believe me?"

"Means I've taken heed of what you said, Miss Miles."

"And what does that mean?" she demanded impatiently.

"That if JJ doesn't have my money when I find him, anybody in this town could have stolen it."

Now she nodded. "That is precisely correct."

The man sitting easy in the saddle and the woman standing so rigidly in front of him at the center of the intersection remained the focus of much silent and anxious attention from certain townspeople who had realized Miss Emma's pronouncement did not end the matter. They strained to overhear what the two were saying, but could not. They did see, however, a sudden change in the attitude of Elizabeth Miles. She became less tense in her stance and the lines of her expression softened a little.

"Some who are out of town, too," she said.

"I'm including the company men, lady."

"I mean Ham Linn and the other members of the company, Edge. Between us we lost twice as much as you did. And, like you, we won't be reimbursed when Mr. Sheldon returns to town."

"The whole bunch?"

She nodded and sighed. "It seems I was wrong about them sitting around and complaining all night. They did decide to do something. Appears that at first light this morning they hitched the wagon and left town to try to get our money back." She shrugged. "But perhaps that was after one of them stole your money, Edge. Thought you ought to know."

"Obliged."

She swung around and strode back to the porch. Went up on to it and watched as Edge turned his horse and heeled the animal into a slow walk toward the northwestern stretch of Pine Street. The slightest of smiles turned up the corners of her mouth as another buzz of excited talk was triggered by the sight of the half-breed leaving town.

Edge was unaware of the secret smile, and the rasping voices quickly faded from his hearing as he rode to the end of the street. The last building on his right had a black-draped display window featuring a marble cross and a sign above reading: H. BALLINGER FUNERAL DIRECTOR.

To one side of the single story building a short, fat, middle-aged man with a round and very red face had already restarted the chore he'd been doing when the bullet hit the bell. He was washing down a shiny black-painted landaulet which had been converted for use as a hearse. He was dressed in soiled work clothes, except for a high-crowned black hat with a veil hanging down from the back brim.

The mortician pretended to be too assiduously engaged in his labor to notice Edge until the half-breed reined in his horse and asked, "Did last night's killings clean you out of caskets?"

The man was sweating from more than just his exertions in the morning sun. "No, sir. I always maintain a goodly stock. There's always a ready supply of timber available, of course. More than needs be, really. Ridgeville being such a healthy place to live and there not being so many elderly folks who—"

"If there happens to be an epidemic of fatal disease while I'm away, be obliged if you'd hold one casket back," Edge cut in on the babbling man.

The mortician shook his head and fixed an insecure smile on his fleshy face. "I don't think you have to worry on that score, sir. The Grim Reaper takes very long vacations hereabouts."

"He put in some overtime on the night shift."

The nervous smile was wiped away. "It was terrible, terrible," he said, then went back to work with the wad of rags and bucket of soapy water, a professional frown on his ruddy face.

Edge heeled the mare forward, off the end of the street and out onto the trail that ran into the timberland.

"Oh, sir!"

The rider paused to glance back over his shoulder.

"My cheapest casket comes out at fifteen dollars!"

"Cheapest will do."

The mortician was nervous again under the level gaze of the glinting blue eyes between the narrowed lids. He swallowed hard before he added, "Of course, burial is extra."

"I'll need for the corpse to be buried, feller."

Another gulp. "Say twenty dollars all in, sir?"

"Explains why you're in a dying business," Edge growled.

"I'm afraid I fail to understand you, sir."

"At your prices, I figure the cost of living has to be cheaper."

Chapter Five

IT was pleasant to ride through the cool, pine-scented shade of the trail that curved gently away from the northwest and headed south. Apart from the spurs that angled off toward lumber camps—some abandoned and others still being worked—it was the only trail in this area of the Beartooth Mountains. Edge was backtracking over familiar ground. He had ridden along the valley bottom for two days before reaching its dead end at Ridgeville.

Before this he had been in the saddle for many weeks. On trails and across country, moving northward without haste through the eastern ridges of the Continental Divide. Just drifting, with no destination in mind. Sleeping under the stars most nights, with the occasional luxury of a bed in an isolated community where he stopped over to replenish his supplies. Buying what he needed from a bankroll which was comprised largely of reward money, earned as a result of an earlier run-in with violent trouble that had not been of his making.

And it was the balance of this reward money

that had been stolen from him during the night. The larger part of it by far, because the needs of this man called Edge were few—just a good horse, serviceable gear, and sufficient food for himself and for his mount. Everything else was surplus—acceptable but never essential.

It had not always been so; but even during his formative years the seeds of the kind of man he was destined to become had begun to germinate. When he lived on an Iowa farmstead with his Mexican father, Scandinavian mother, and younger brother Jamie. When he was the quiet one in the family, doing his schoolwork and his share of the chores to the best of his ability and never desiring anything that was not available and affordable. Then, after the death of his parents, he had accepted the responsibility of running the place and taking care of Jamie. He dealt as efficiently with the infrequent intrusions of man-made trouble as he'd dealt with the seasonal work in the fields.

When the War Between the States came, he felt compelled to fight for the Union and left Jamie—crippled by a shooting accident—to take care of the farmstead. First as a lieutenant and then as a captain, he rode the eastern battlegrounds and quickly discovered a latent capacity to kill without compunction and to survive without remorse.

His name was then Josiah C. Hedges, and when the war was won he rode immediately back to Iowa. He was eager to shed his uniform and military rank, to become a farmer again, and to forget the deadly skills that war had taught him. Hopeful, perhaps, that the darker side of himself would be buried and remain so.

But it was not to be.

Six men he had led and fought alongside during most of the war reached the farmstead ahead of him. And left it a burnt-out shell, with the mutilated body of Jamie as buzzard meat in the yard.

In tracking down and making the killers of his kid brother pay for their crime, Josiah C. Hedges became a wanted man named Edge. And started out on the trail that had brought him to the Montana timber town of Ridgeville. A trail that had zigzagged through many of the states of the Union, across most of its territories, and into Mexico.

On only one occasion had he wanted, to the exclusion of all other considerations, something that was not essential to his survival. A woman for his wife. But that time was far in his past now. So too was his need to keep on the move as an outlaw, for he had been granted an amnesty for that old killing.

But he was too set in the ways of a lone drifter, and as inevitably as he was driven to ride the aimless and endless trail, so he was dogged by violence and the need to make use of his ruthless killing skills. He no longer paused to reflect on why this should be so. Nor did he seek to justify his actions to himself anymore. He killed to stay alive and any man or woman who stood between him and this most fundamental of ambitions was on borrowed time.

In this instance, as the half-breed rode down the tree-fringed trail toward the sawmill of the Montana Lumber Company, the situation was clear-cut. In his saddlebags were supplies that could be stretched to last him no more than a week. And somebody had stolen the money which would have kept him fed for a lot longer. Without food, he would die. *Ergo,* the thief was going to die.

The sawmill was situated in a large clearing and was comprised of a long, barnlike building on the bank of the creek with a line of smaller buildings to either side. The latter formed a kind of courtyard which was open to the trail. A stack on either end of the mill belched smoke, and steam hissed from two engines and drifted across the creek. Pistons thudded and the blades of the bandsaws screeched as they cut through recently felled trees. Heavy log trucks and flatbed wagons were parked in the courtyard, the teams in the traces. Men were unloading trunks brought in from the scattered camps from some and loading sawed planks for nearby storage or shipment to the south on others.

The men who were busy at this backbreaking work showed no sign that they saw the rider coming in off the trail. Until a steam whistle sounded and the activity was suddenly halted. Then those outside were joined by several men from within the sawmill, and all of them headed for a long shack that was obviously the mess hall.

He was spotted then by a few of the men, who spread the word to others. He recognized some from the show in the Long Pine Saloon last night. But nobody called a greeting or even nodded in his direction as he reined the mare to a halt and swung down from the saddle. He led his mount to the front of a shack that had the company name painted on a board on the roof and the word

45

OFFICE on its door. The steady hiss of steam escaping through the safety valves of the idling engines sounded pleasant after the cacophony of noise when the mill was in operation.

As he hitched his horse to a log truck, Edge could see a man working at a desk through the single window of the office. The man seemed oblivious to the break in routine outside. Edge pushed open the door without knocking.

"Something I can do for you?" the man asked tersely without looking up from a column of figures he was totaling. He sounded like he was overworked and behind schedule, ready to be angry if the interruption was not justified.

"I figure your company has got some good maps of this part of the country," Edge said as he came into the small, cluttered office and kicked the door closed behind him.

The man abandoned his clerical chore and jerked up his head, surprised that his visitor was not an employee. Edge recalled seeing him sitting, without female company, in the audience at the saloon last night. He was no more than twenty-five, tall and slightly built, with sandy-colored hair and a pale, freckled face. He was afraid of the half-breed and caught his breath when his visitor came close to the desk to reach a section of wall to which a contour map was pinned.

"Really, you can't come in here and just . . ."

Edge had taken the makings from a shirt pocket and was rolling a cigarette as he scanned the small-scale map of the entire valley. Now he glanced down at where the clerk was half-turned

46

in the chair behind the desk, looking nervously up at him.

"I just did, feller. You have any large-scale maps which break down this whole area into sections?" He reached down to his holstered gun and the clerk flinched back into his chair. But the move by Edge was simply made to strike a match on the butt of the Colt.

"Certainly we have such maps, sir. But they are company-made and company property. With Mr. Sheldon gone to Casper I'm not sure I can—"

"Where are they? In the desk? In one of these closets?"

He kicked a leg of the desk and waved a hand to encompass the line of file cabinets along a side wall of the office. And as he did this, he glimpsed through the window a line of six big-built men advancing across the yard. Grim-faced men, each swinging an ax at his side. A falling ax, with a double head and a four-foot-long haft.

"Please, I wouldn't like for there to be trouble while Mr. Sheldon was away," the clerk blurted, blinking rapidly.

"So just show me the maps and tell those fellers with the axes to go finish their coffee break, feller. And I'll leave just as soon as I've found out what I need to know."

Two men halted outside the window and peered into the office. The clerk blinked more furiously than before as he looked back at them. Then he vented a squeal of alarm when the door was kicked open and two more men with axes stepped over the threshold.

"Is this guy givin' you trouble, Fred?" one of them growled as both took a double-handed grip

47

on their axes, bringing them up to hold them across the base of their bellies.

"I don't think so," the clerk blurted, and started to chew on the side of an ink-stained forefinger. "He wants to look at company maps. And with Mr. Sheldon away, I don't know if I should—"

"Why, mister?"

The men outside the window, the two on the threshold, and the other two who remained just outside the doorway had all been in the Lone Pine Saloon last night. Three of them in the group at the bar counter where Edge had stood. But none gave any sign that he recognized the half-breed. Their spokesman was a giant of about six feet seven inches who weighed close to three hundred pounds and had dark-stained flesh that looked to be as pitted as the bark of the trees he worked with.

"Because I'm out a lot of money I need to get back, feller."

"I heard you didn't have your cash in the bank?"

"You heard right. Which was none of your business. Just like this."

"Mighty uppity for a guy with a little bitty revolver against all of us, ain't he, George?" one of the men outside the doorway growled.

"Please, no trouble!" Fred urged.

"Ain't against anybody unless he stole my bankroll," Edge said. "But I'm ready to kill anyone who gets in the way of me getting to the thief."

A series of sneers and grunts greeted this, and gnarled hands took a tighter hold on the axes. Fred came up from his chair and took the chewed finger out of his mouth. He could not control the rapid blinking of his eyes.

"Look, this is ridiculous! Mr. Edge, if you are prepared to give me a reason I can accept for wanting to look at our maps, then I am prepared to—"

"Hold it, Caxton," George cut in. "Me and the boys ain't ready to believe anythin' just because this stranger says it's so."

A man at the window snarled, "And where do you get off, stranger, sayin' it ain't none of our business you comin' in here and scarin' the shit outta Fred Caxton?"

The clerk started to shake his head in a tacit denial of the fact that he was afraid, while his freckled face showed that he was . . . but of the situation rather than of Edge.

The half-breed took the part-smoked cigarette from the corner of his mouth and lowered it to his side before he parted his thumb and forefinger to drop it to the floor. Nobody in the office or peering in from outside saw the component parts of the move that followed. For the hand which had released the cigarette was in full view. Yet, less than a second later, it could be seen fisted around the butt of a leveled revolver. What happened between took place in a blur of speed.

"Oh, sweet Jesus," Fred Caxton squeezed out from his constricted throat. And thrust his arms high above his head, his eyes snapping closed.

The two men at the window threw themselves to either side of it. Likewise those beyond the threshold of the doorway. While George and the other lumberman inside the office stood rooted to the floor, knowing there could be no escape if

49

Edge elected to swing the Colt to aim at them and squeeze the trigger.

"Wasn't my intention to scare anybody," the half-breed drawled. And angled the gun slightly as he thrust it out from his right hip and brought his left hand across the front of his body. "Or to kill anybody except the feller that stole my money." The Colt was aimed at a spot on the lintel of the door. He curled his right forefinger more snugly to the trigger and used the heel of his left hand to fan the hammer. The bullets left the muzzle on a rising trajectory and cracked between the heads of George and the slightly shorter man on the other side of the doorway. "But, like I said, I will kill the feller gets between me and the thief."

The men flanking the doorway instinctively leaned to the side as the stream of rapid-fire bullets streaked between them. Expressing the dread of violent death for the brief period during which the Colt was fanned. Then, in the first moment of silence after the final gunshot, as nostrils flared to the stench of black powder smoke drifting across the office, George and his partner twisted their heads around to stare at the area of the blasted door lintel. They saw that the bullets were imbedded in a patch of scarred wood no more than three inches in diameter.

"He's emptied his friggin' gun! Let's get the sonofabitch!" a man yelled from outside the shack. But horror was inscribed upon his weather-beaten features when he appeared on the threshold and pulled up short.

What he, like George and the other man, saw was that Edge had raised the Colt and pushed it out to the side. To press the muzzle gently against the side of Fred Caxton's head, just above the quivering clerk's left ear.

"You were right, Fred," the half-breed said evenly. "This is ridiculous, isn't it? Me needing to waste shells firing at a wall. And now you being in the firing line. You want to tell these fellers that's the only part that adds up?"

The clerk flapped his mouth, but only low and strangled sounds emerged.

"What you talkin' about, stranger?" the towering George asked.

"Quinn's wrong, George," the other lumberman in the shack explained after taking another look at the bullets imbedded in the lintel. "He only pumped five shells into the friggin' wall. That's a six-shooter he's got, so Fred's just a finger pull away from gettin' his head holed."

"But he won't get away with it, Fry," Quinn said, excitement back in his tone. "Here, give it me, Colley!"

The burst of gunfire had brought the rest of the sawmill workers out of the mess hall. But it was not the sight of these men gathered into a close-knit group as they advanced on the office that gave Quinn renewed confidence. It was the Winchester rifle that was tossed at him. And which he caught clumsily after releasing his hold on the falling ax.

"You aim that at me, you kill me with it!" Edge rasped, his tone as icy cold as the glittering stare of his eyes. "If you don't, you're dead!"

The stance of the half-breed was suddenly a perfect match for his voice and the look on his lean face. Until this moment there had been no

51

mistaking the menace of what he was doing. Even though there was a certain nonchalance about his attitude, as though he were not taking the situation too seriously. Like he did not think it probable he would be pushed to carry out his threat. But now he was suddenly rigid on the surface—like stone. There was something about him which subtly suggested to one of the lumbermen that he was the very opposite of rigid underneath—was poised to react with fluid speed should Quinn ignore the warning.

"Horseshit!" Quinn snarled. And folded the lever of the Winchester away from the base of the frame.

It was the half-breed's own rifle. Taken by Colley—one of the men at the window—from the boot hung on the saddle of the mare. Edge saw this at the moment Quinn caught the gun. And it was undoubtedly this fact that aroused a colder than usual rage within him at the prospect of being a target for the rifle. For it had been the family rifle, and he and Jamie had played with it as children. The rifle which had exploded a bullet that should not have been in the breech. And made the younger brother a cripple for the rest of his tragically short life.

Edge whirled, arcing the Colt away from the side of the head of the trembling clerk. He focused it on Quinn as the lumberman just outside the doorway snapped the lever back into place, the hammer cocked behind a live shell.

The towering George remained rooted to the spot, as before, staring in amazement at the speed of the half-breed.

Unlike George, Fry did not.

52

He had started his move before Quinn gave his answer to Edge and had partly turned away from the half-breed as the Colt muzzle was taken away from the clerk's head. Barely a second after Edge aimed the revolver at Quinn, Fry had his back to Edge and was lunging over the treshhold. The ax fell from his hands, freeing them to reach for, grip the Winchester, and wrench it from the grasp of the enraged Quinn.

"Everybody friggin' hold it!" Fry screamed above the obscenities that Quinn was snarling amid a spray of spittle. "This whole friggin' thing is crazy and nobody has to get killed here!"

"Oh, sweet Jesus," the clerk murmured, keeping his arms thrust high above his head.

Edge was just a sliver of time away from squeezing the trigger of the Colt. Which now would have blasted the final bullet into the broad back of the man named Fry. And for another fraction of a second that seemed to go on for much longer, it was as if the effort required to keep from firing the revolver drained him of every iota of energy.

But then a sense of reality was restored, dissipating the sense of nightmarish hallucination which had briefly taken a hold on almost everyone in the vicinity.

The half-breed's tone of voice was even and matter-of-fact when he drawled, "That's you, me, and Fry, Fred. But it's getting tougher to win votes for our way of thinking."

As he spoke he brought the acrid-smelling Colt up to the side of his face and began to scratch his cheek with the foresight.

Fry called to the group of lumbermen. "It's

okay, you guys! No blood and there ain't gonna be none! It's time we got back to work!"

The scowling Quinn was still cursing, but under his breath now. George was scratching his head as he expressed a frown of perplexity. He maintained a firm double-handed grip on his ax as he continued to eye Edge. "I don't get it, Phil," he said at last, as Quinn and the other three men immediately outside the shack turned and followed the large group toward the sawmill. "It was your idea to come brace this guy."

Phil Fry reentered the shack, holding the Winchester around the barrel with one hand, the stock dragging behind him. He did not close the door after him. "Get them arms down and put your ass back on your chair, Fred," he growled at the clerk. Then he swung the Winchester upward so that the stock banged down on the top of the paper-littered desk and pushed it toward Edge. "There you go, mister. Your property. Let's start this over. Without anyone gettin' hot under the collar unless there's good reason."

Fred Caxton had done as instructed and started to blink again and chew the side of his forefinger. The massively built George remained perplexed. Phil Fry, a head shorter and a hundred pounds lighter than George, looked at Edge expectantly.

The half-breed said, "Obliged," as the two steam engines were set to work again, spinning the bandsaws to tear into the logs with high-pitched screeching sounds. These masked the much lower sounds Edge made as he emptied the Colt of spent shellcases and fed fresh bullets into the chambers.

Fry waited impatiently for him to finish and

then demanded as the Colt was slid into the holster, "You gonna say why you want to look at the company maps?"

"And you have to allow it is our business, sir," Caxton added quickly. "But as I said earlier, if you are able to offer me a reasonable . . ."

Edge had taken out the makings and rolled a cigarette. When the cylinder was completed and the paper licked, he cut in on the eager-to-please clerk. "There's no sweat about that, feller. You and me would have gotten along fine if man-mountain there and the rest hadn't busted in on us." He struck a match on the butt of his holstered revolver and lit the cigarette. "You would have asked and I'd have told you. Just like now. I want to look at the maps to see if I can figure out the most likely areas in this part of the country where the Campbell bunch might be holed up."

"Some of us figured . . ." George started.

"You're goin' after the Campbells?" Fry interrupted.

Edge blew out some tobacco smoke on a sigh. "No, feller. General opinion around Ridgeville is that John James took my bankroll. When he rode out of town, though, he claimed he was going after the Campbells because they killed the sheriff."

"It's what JJ said he planned to do right enough," George allowed, and looked pleased that he was at last able to make a contribution to the exchange.

Fry looked miserable and chewed the inside of his cheek for a few moments. Then he grunted with disgust and growled, "Shit, mister. Seems we had you figured all wrong. But you gotta admit we had cause for suspicion."

"Why do I have to do that, feller?"

"Hell, near the whole town was in the saloon when the bank was raided. And you was the only man in there armed. A stranger with a mean look to you. When you look at it from our point of view, you gotta see how you could've been one of the bunch. Planted in the saloon to see no one interfered with what was happenin' over to the bank!"

"You just figure that out today, feller? Or did it . . ."

"Don't you go usin' that tone of voice to us, mister!" George snarled. "That makes out like you think we ain't got no guts!"

"Easy," Fry urged. "Let's do like I said and not get hot under the collar."

"But, Phil. This gunslinger acts like he figures we're—"

"What he figures about us is nothin' to us, George," Fry snapped, and the anger in his tone was emphasized in his eyes as he looked at the half-breed, then jerked his head. "Shit, mister. You don't need no map to find where the friggin' Campbell bunch are at. Come on outside of here."

He went to the door, stooping to retrieve his discarded ax as he did so. George followed him and then Edge, the Winchester canted to his right shoulder.

The lumbermen who were loading and unloading the wagons continued their work after glancing at the front of the shack and seeing that all was well.

"See them twin peaks over there, mister?" Fry said, his right arm raised, his forefinger pointing to the west.

56

The half-breed looked in this direction and nodded.

"That's Cloud Pass. Ain't no trail that leads to it and there's some real rough country to cross to reach it. But with them two ridges stickin' up the way they do, you'll always know which direction to head in."

"Take you a day or two and a night to reach the place, mister," George added as Phil Fry turned to move away from the shack. "And you better make the most of the time. On account of when you get there, it'll all be run out for you." The big man spat and swung around to follow Fry toward the sawmill.

Edge looked again to the west where the ground rose gently to form one side of the broad, shallow valley of the Little Creek. It seemed from where he stood to be entirely covered with Ponderosa pines and Douglas firs, a green, featureless expanse with just the distant rocky peaks to mar the otherwise smooth line of the horizon. He heard a sound behind him and asked without turning, "How can they be so sure the Campbell bunch are holed up in Cloud Pass, Fred?"

"Morning, noon, and suppertime of most days, we can see the smoke of their cooking fires, sir," the clerk answered. "Anyone in Ridgeville could have told you the same thing."

The half-breed went to unhitch the mare from the wheel of the truck and swung up into the saddle. "Never occurred to me it would be that simple, feller. But town business ain't mine so I got no need to ask anything else. Obliged to you for your help."

Caxton blinked up at the mounted man and

frowned as he searched his mind for words to express what he felt was necessary before Edge touched his heels to the flanks of the mare. Finally he blurted, "Look, mister, if somebody was going to give back exactly what was stolen from you, would you risk your life and put your home and family in danger going after the people that robbed you?"

Edge pursed his thin lips, nodded, and answered through his teeth, "You bet your ass I would, feller."

The clerk started to chew on the side of his inky finger again, something akin to shame showing in his rapidly blinking eyes. The half-breed was aware of many pairs of anxious eyes watching the front of the shack. But all the lumbermen pretended to be fully engaged in their chores when he glanced around him.

"Well, it doesn't apply in your case, does it?" Caxton said quickly and defensively. "It's just that crazy old drunk JJ you're going after. And when you catch up with him, he won't be no trouble for a man like you to deal with."

Edge briefly fingered the scab-roughened skin of his left temple and drew back his lips to show a smile that failed to inject any warmth into the glittering slits of his eyes. "Just so long as I don't allow his liquor to go to my head again, Fred."

Chapter Six

EDGE rode away from the sawmill and into the timber without concern for the attitude of the men of Ridgeville that the young clerk had expressed. Nor did he reflect, as the thud of steam-driven pistons and the shriek of sawteeth through timber faded behind him, upon whether he had chosen the correct course of action to get back what had been stolen from him.

For his mind had been fully made up when he rode out of town after listening to Miss Emma and Elizabeth Miles, and he had heard nothing at the sawmill to cause him to doubt his decision. So his mind was as blank as his expression as he veered between the trees to left and right, moving up the constant gentle slope, the thud of the mare's hooves muted by a thick carpet of pine needles.

He rode without haste throughout the morning and rested himself and his mount at midday when he had a meal of jerked beef washed down with canteen water. It was very quiet in the forest and the air was chilly. When he set off again he rode hunched inside a sheepskin coat, the collar turned up to brush against his hat.

As they had been during the morning, his senses were alert only to the extent that was normal for him when he traveled through unfamiliar country—hearing and eyesight attuned to pick up the first sign of unknown danger. Still, they were backed up by a finely honed feeling for the presence of a menace before it could be heard or seen, and behind his apparently relaxed attitude, he was poised to react instantly to the unexpected. As he rode the slow-moving mare, his body was as tense as it had been in the company office—before the man named Quinn unwittingly touched one of the few raw nerves of the man named Edge. His progress during the afternoon was much slower than in the morning since the terrain became as difficult as the massively built George had warned him. The timbered side of the valley was not nearly as evenly surfaced as it appeared from the sawmill by the creek.

Rock escarpments reared up along the path to the twin peaks. Sometimes a ravine seemed to offer a way, only to dead-end blindly. More often, impenetrable thickets of prickly brush forced him to take wide detours. But the fact that the two ridges which flanked Cloud Pass were seldom in sight through the towering trees was never a handicap. For he had abandoned his original notion to make directly for the pass and was content to know that as long as he was constantly on an upgrade, he was getting closer to his objective.

He made camp as soon as darkness started to drape the mountains and lit a small fire to boil water for coffee and cook bacon and beans. As soon as the fire had served its purpose, he doused it and bedded down in his blankets. The Winchester, with a bullet in the breech but the hammer not cocked, shared his bed—his right hand fisted around the frame.

While he lay, waiting for sleep, he was aware for the first time in many hours of the dull ache under his skull. And while he hovered on the brink of sleep, he was visited by a stray thought that maybe he was suffering from the concussion Doc Hunter had warned of. That it was hampering his powers of reason and causing him to act illogically—or, at least, to follow a course of action which was foreign to his nature.

Then sleep came, untroubled from within and undisturbed from without, until the birds of the forest commenced their dawn chorus. They roused Edge to a cold world in which the gray light of early sunrise had replaced the blackness of night.

He woke to instant awareness and total recall. He knew he had bedded down at the mouth of a ravine which offered the only way up the valley toward the pass, unless he wanted to backtrack at least a mile to locate the start of an alternative route. His head ached a little but did not thud as he sat up, pulled on his boots, and put on his hat. Then he spat out the taste of yesterday, drank a little water from a canteen, and splashed some on his face. Rolled and lit a cigarette, smoked it as he packed his gear and saddled the mare. Climbed astride the horse and heeled her into the ravine. Meanwhile the sun rose behind him and punched narrow shafts of cool light down through the trees.

The ravine, despite its thickly wooded rims was

61

not a blind one, yet he still had to dismount and lead the mare by the reins up the treacherous shale slope to get out of it. Small rocks skittered out from under the feet of the man and the hooves of the horse as they climbed. Edge sweated with the exertion and the animal snorted with unease at almost every step.

The horse became quieted down when they again reached firm ground at the top of the steep and slippery incline. The half-breed ran the back of a hand across his sticky forehead and peered along the natural path that led northwestward among the timber. He sensed, a useless part of a second before he heard a sound, that the noisy climb up over the shale had attracted dangerous attention.

The sound he heard was metallic—the unmistakable click of a gun hammer being thumbed back. But he revealed no sign of his awareness of being watched as he turned toward the horse and made as if to remount—sliding his left foot into the stirrup and reaching for the saddlehorn with his left hand. This put his back to the area where the watcher lurked, and during the moment he was in this position, every pore in his body pumped sweat and the muscles between his shoulder blades bunched the flesh in expectation of a searing bullet. The obedient mare stood still, sideways-on to the top of the ravine end and the start of the ten-foot-wide pathway.

Edge continued the charade of swinging up into the saddle for a half-second more—taking a firm grip of the horn and pushing clear of the ground with his right foot. Then heard the crack of a dry twig. About the same twenty feet away as the cocking of the gun, but on the other side.

Now the half-breed powered into speed. He arced his trailing right leg high as he applied greater leverage with his left foot in the stirrup. While his left hand wrenched at the horn and his right fisted around the frame of the booted Winchester.

"Get him, he's seen us!" a woman shrieked.

A fusillade of gunshots exploded in the immediate wake of her shrill words.

Edge's left leg was arcing through the same curve as the right now, having kicked clear of the stirrup. His sole contact with the suddenly skittish horse was now his left hand on the horn—which acted as the pivot for his swing up and over the frightened animal. The rifle was clear of the boot as the gunfire sounded.

Edge had released his grip on the saddlehorn and was struggling to keep from rolling onto his back in mid-air when the mare reared.

The first shots had been fired wildly, the men behind the guns surprised by the half-breed's sudden move and responding instinctively to the command of the woman. Now, after there had been time for fresh rounds to be levered and rotated in front of the firing pins, the rearing horse was between the gun muzzles and the free-falling target.

The mare returned to all fours and two shots were blasted beneath her belly. One of the bullets came close enough to splice through the long hair that waved above the head of the half-breed. As he hit the ground with his thighs, belly, chest, and upper arms, he clutched the Winchester high and safe from impact.

The crash sent the air in his lungs rushing out between his clenched teeth with a snarled obscenity instead of a grunt of pain. Tears blurred his vision and he wrenched his teeth apart to suck in more air as he quietly cursed the hampering pain and sought to ignore it. He forced himself to roll off the firm ground at which the mare was scraping and stamping and onto the unstable shale.

"I got him! I sure as hell did, Fay!"

Edge clearly heard these shouted words of triumph. But then he heard nothing except the din of the rockslide that he caused and was a part of for almost half the hundred-foot distance to the bottom of the ravine.

He would have gone all the way down had he given in to the demands of his punished body. But he had suffered worse many times in the long and harsh past and had learned how to suppress such needs for self-indulgence, how to summon up what was necessary to induce a state of mind over matter. As he ceased to roll and turned his body so that he was slithering—feet first—down the slope, it was relatively easy to absorb the buffeting. To feel the pain, but to use it instead of simply succumbing to it.

Each rock he slid over, each rock that bounced off him, each rock that burned him with friction and smacked into him, acted to steady his resolve to kill those who were responsible for this new agony. And if he were to succeed in this, there would be even less opportunity to allow himself the luxury of surrendering to the onslaught of pain. So he dug in the toes of his boots, his kneecaps and the points of his elbows and felt the warmth of blood on his arms and legs. Through his tear-blurred vision he saw traces of red on the gray rocks.

His downslide slowed and finally came to a halt perhaps five seconds after it had begun. And he paused for no more than a second while small rocks continued to roll and skitter about him. Sprawled out full-length.

Then he pushed himself up to his badly skinned knees and elbows and thumbed back the hammer of the Winchester. Tilted back his head to turn his sweat-sheened, heavily bristled, agony-contorted face toward the top of the slope. Squeezed his eyes tightly closed and then snapped them wide open to flick the salt moisture away from their lids. Cracked them to the narrowest of glittering slits and altered his mouth from a grimace to something close to a grin—but not close enough for the merest suggestion of evil humor to detract from the bottomless brutality of his eyes.

Edge started back up the treacherous slope, pushing with his feet and dragging with his elbows. Rasping air in through his flared nostrils and whistling it out between his clenched teeth. These sounds were loud in his own ears, but were otherwise masked by the constant pounding of tumbling rocks that his upward progress dislodged.

He held to a line in the center of the slope, ignoring the brush that grew in thick clumps six feet to either side. A warning was registering in the back of his mind that this was the wrong thing to do, but he rejected it, too eager to kill for caution to have any appeal.

65

His horse was now calm. She stood in the cool morning sunlight with ears and eyes alert yet without any sign of tension.

"So go check it out, John," a man said.

"Reckon I'll wait until that racket is finished," John answered.

"Christ, what was Craig thinking of, sending a couple of yellow bellies like you to pick me up?" the woman called Fay said sourly. "Even if he wasn't hit, he ain't gonna be no picture of health after tumbling down the damn hill, is he?"

Edge had halted his agonizing and awkward climb when the first man spoke, the words sounding clearly through the diminishing noise of the sliding shale. He was some ten feet below the point where the mare stood on the firm and level ground and as he froze to the sound of the voice, he allowed himself to utter a low grunt of disgust. Self-disgust that he had not guarded against impulsive anger, that he had moved recklessly along the line that was the shortest distance between two points to close with the enemy, instead of making for cover and taking the time to plan his counterattack.

Fresh sweat drenched him from head to toe as he briefly reflected on whether this would be the final mistake. If he would pay with his life for once more not taking heed of the lessons that experience had taught him so often—many times during the war and along several of the trails he had ridden since then. That anger, in every instance, was a self-indulgent emotion that a man in danger could not afford to feel.

Then, as the other man spoke and the woman revealed the fact that there was just herself and two escorts, the killer grin returned to the lean, dark-skinned face of the half-breed. For a moment he held still on all fours.

Then he eased up onto his haunches and held the rifle in his left hand, finger curved to the trigger and stock wedged between his side and his blood-sticky elbow. He drew the Colt from the holster, clicked back the hammer, and with the barrels of both guns parallel, drew beads on the shoulder and hindquarters of the docile mare.

The final rolling rock skittered to a stop at the base of the slope.

Booted feet were set down on the track beyond the horse, the muted sounds of the three people moving on the pine-needle ground covering.

John rasped, "He could be playin' possum, Arnie."

"Maybe."

"Christ, you guys trying to talk some courage into yourselves!" Fay snarled. She surged forward so fast that she spooked the mare into lunging out of her path.

Arnie yelled: "No, stay back!"

John snapped at the same time: "Grab her!"

"Take your hands off . . . damn you!"

Edge saw her first, just her head above the top of the slope. But it was turned to the side to direct a look of outrage at one of her escorts, so she had no chance to see him before she was jerked back. She squealed with alarm and perhaps pain as she thudded to the ground.

The half-breed powered himself upright at that moment, rasping out a curse that was part triumph and part response to the bolt of pain the sudden movement drove through him.

67

Two men with Frontier Colts in their hands stared at him with horror-widened eyes, each of them frozen in a half-crouch. One had been dragging the woman back from the top of the slope and the other looking to see why she had squealed.

"Shit!" the taller, thinner man in his mid-forties groaned.

"Sonofa . . ." the other man, who was ten years younger, started to bark.

· Fay had been sent sprawling on her back. Now she folded sharply up into a sitting position and murmured, "Well, I'll be damned."

Edge squeezed the triggers of both guns simultaneously and shot Arnie and John in their chests as they made to swing their guns toward him. Heart shots, the bullets tearing through flesh and passing between lower ribs on a rising trajectory to penetrate the vital organs. Not bringing death to the victims until they had a second in which to realize it was the end for them.

The elder man, who received the revolver bullet, simply straightened up, swayed to the side, and fell, firing his gun at the ground in front of him. The higher velocity of the bullet from the Winchester lifted the other man an inch or so off the ground and hurled him violently backward. He tried to bring his hands up to the blossoming stain on his shirt front, but never made it. His gun fell from his nerveless grasp without being fired.

Edge swung up the rifle to his left shoulder. He had the revolver hammer thumbed back and the gun aimed at the baby-doll face of the woman before the men were stretched out and motionless on the ground to either side of her.

She had a brief moment of terror when she saw them blasted to death, but now she smiled. And Edge could see no sign that she had to force the expression across her pale-skinned, overpainted features. "You wouldn't shoot a lady, would you, mister?" she asked.

Edge had planted his feet squarely on the shale when he came erect to trigger shots at the men. And it seemed as if every muscle in his tall frame had been locked to keep his aim steady and absorb the shock of the recoils. But he did not trust himself to retain his balance on the slope for much longer. So he used some precious reserves of stamina to free his knotted muscles and make them carry him to the top of the slope. There he stood on the area of ground vacated by his horse and willed himself to stay upright and not to sway. He was aware that he was dangerously close to finally giving in to the pain that assaulted him. And giving in would mean stretching out on the ground and closing his eyes. To invite sleep or unconsciousness. Just like the two fellers on the ground in front of him . . .

"I knew you couldn't, mister," the woman said. And her voice seemed to come from the bottom of a deep, echoing mine shaft. "Hey, why don't you take the weight off and rest for a while, uh? You look done in."

Her voice suddenly sounded normal. And at the instant Edge heard her, he recalled that he had just killed the two men. Men who had been urged on to kill him by this woman.

He had not known that his eyes had briefly closed at the thought. Now he cracked them open again and drew back from the brink of a tantalizingly inviting state of torpor. His glittering gaze and the black muzzle of the Colt searched for and found the raven-haired, round-faced, full-lipped, and blue-eyed woman named Fay.

Who was no longer sitting between two dead men and smiling beguilingly at a live one. Rather, she had fallen to her hands and knees and was reaching for the revolver that Arnie or John had dropped. Her head was screwed around so that she could watch the half-breed, who a moment before had seemed about to keel over and pass out. But he had pulled himself together and now Fay expressed deep-seated terror as the ice-blue slits of his eyes trapped her gaze.

"You can't kill me, mister, I'm Craig Campbell's woman!" she shrieked. And slid her left hand an inch along the ground—so that the tips of her fingers were only half that distance away from contact with the discarded gun.

"He got a line to the Almighty?" Edge asked evenly.

"Uh?" The woman was slightly less afraid and she stayed her hand from moving closer to the revolver. She obviously considered the half-breed's willingness to talk a good sign. "He's the only feller I know with the power to make people immortal." She tried another smile and this one did show signs of strain at the sides of the painted mouth and eyes. "Hell, mister, I'm not that. And if heaven does hand out those kind of favors, I reckon I'm right at the back of the line. Me living the kind of life that I do."

"Did," Edge said.

"Uh?"

She was puzzled and just vaguely anxious for a

moment. Then she realized what he meant by the monosyllabic remark. And a mixture of horror, rage, and despair wiped the fake smile from her face, as she thrust her left hand forward, fingers clawing at the Colt and her mouth gaping wide to vent a scream.

Edge squeezed the trigger of his revolver. He heard the crack of the bullet leaving the muzzle, but felt a fresh explosion of pain in the hand that fired the gun. He saw the Colt spin away from his grasp as another gunshot reached his ears.

"Don't move a muscle, bitch!" a man shrieked.

Edge swung the Winchester down from his shoulder, bringing up his stinging right hand to fist around the barrel. He felt a new surge of rage as his pain-dulled mind finally realized that the Colt had been blasted away by another shot at the moment he fired it.

He saw that the woman was frozen like a statue. Still on her hands and knees, with one of her hands fisted around the butt of the Colt she had so desperately wanted to reach. His bullet had missed her and her attention was held by another man now. Directly in front of her, but among the timber and out of sight of the half-breed.

Edge knew from the way his Colt had fallen that whoever had shot it out of his grasp was on the other side of the track. And he turned in this direction as he worked the lever action of the repeater. Knowing in the back of his pain- and anger-ravaged brain that the bullet which had hit his gun could just as easily have been aimed into his body.

"Please don't do anything hasty, Mr. Edge,"

Hamilton Linn warned excitedly in his booming voice. "It is only I and my fellow actors."

The elderly and slightly-built man emerged from behind a tree some fifteen feet from where Edge stood. He was wearing his cream-colored duster with a charred bullet hole in the left pocket and was carrying his black derby in one hand. His other hand was empty, so it wasn't he who had shot the gun out of the half-breed's grasp. He was smiling brightly.

"Scene one in this play is all."

The actor's smile became a gleeful laugh. "That is most amusing, Mr. Edge!" He clapped his hands just once. "Come, boys and girls. Everybody out of the wings and show yourselves."

It was the eighteen-year-old boy with the feminine good looks who had caused Fay to hold so still, with a Winchester to back up his snarled command. And he continued to aim the rifle at her, angling it down from his narrow shoulder as he emerged on to the track. A scared-looking middle-aged man toting a double-barrel shotgun and a plain girl of twenty or so also came out of the trees on that side.

Like Edge, the bewildered Fay looked away from these toward two other members of the Linn Players who appeared from the timber to flank the smiling man. Another man of about thirty, who was no taller than five feet but had a muscular build. And a taller woman of the same age. The man had a single shot Spencer carbine held at arm's length at his side. While the woman had a two-handed grip on what seemed to be an army-model Colt with a custom-made barrel at least twelve inches long. She held the massive revolver at the base of her belly, the long barrel hanging downward. And she hung her head to look in the same direction just before Edge's glittering eye could meet her gaze.

The half-breed made a conscious effort to force his rage back into a tight, ice-cold ball at the pit of his stomach. He glanced back and forth across the trail and recognized each actor and actress in turn.

"Forgive us for surprising you in such a highly dramatic manner, Mr. Edge," Linn boomed, still smiling brightly while the other members of his company remained tense or afraid. "It seems, though, to give credence to the words of the Bard that . . ."

"Jesus," Fay rasped, letting go of the Colt and shifting back into a sitting position on the track between the two dead men. She gazed up at Edge. "Am I going crazy or are these people for real?"

". . . that all the world's a stage and . . ." Linn tryed to continue.

Edge sloped the Winchester back up to his shoulder and spat a globule of saliva at the ground in front of him before he sighed and said to the woman, "Sure seems to have got started as one crazy 'dais.'"

Chapter Seven

HAMILTON Linn laughed again as he emerged from the forest, followed by the short man who glowered menacingly at Edge and the woman with the long-barrel Colt who continued to hang her head.

"'Dais' as in stage, Mr. Edge. You possess a keen wit, you know."

"Yeah, I'm as sharp as a razor sometimes," the half-breed answered sourly, moving to where his Colt lay on the track. He stooped to pick it up and went toward a tree with an exposed root that provided a makeshift chair. He sat on it and added, "But right now my edge feels a little dulled."

The expertly aimed bullet from the long-barrel Colt had hit the standard model near the cylinder. He hoped the outside dent had not carried through to the inner surface of the barrel, yet he had no particular attachment to the gun and didn't bother to check it out. He rested the rifle across his thighs and tilted the revolver to extract the four unfired bullets from the cylinder.

"Marybelle Melton was formerly with a traveling Wild West show before she joined my company," Hamilton Linn said, a little nervously, his smile strained. "Marksmanship was her particular forte."

"You're good, ma'am," Edge said as he dropped the shells into his shirt pocket and tossed the damaged gun down the shale slope into the ravine.

"Thank you," the sharpshooting woman murmured, without raising her head.

"This is Henry Maguire," Linn went on, indicating the scowling man with the Spencer. "Across the way there is Susie Chase, our ingenue. Young Oliver Strange and Mr. Clarence Gowan. I'm afraid I do not know the name of the young lady to whom young Oliver was so rude a moment ago. And it would appear that there was no time for her to introduce herself to you, Mr. Edge?"

Hamilton Linn was again oozing confidence which seemed to increase by the moment. But the rest of his company was not infected by it. Maguire remained silently bellicose—his aggression directed entirely at Edge—while the others were afraid. Young Strange attempted to conceal this behind a brittle veneer of bravado.

"The name's Fay Lynch, old-timer," the doll-like brunette snarled. "And you better turn me loose right this minute. Or you'll get what that gunslinger's got coming to him." She shifted her hard-eyed gaze from the grinning Linn to Edge, who was rolling a cigarette.

"Pray what is that, young lady?" the actor boomed.

Her attempt at an evil smile was a failure for it

did not fit her softly rounded features. "Nobody guns down a couple of the Campbell bunch and lives for long afterwards. And if you don't turn me loose, actor, you and your bunch will regret it. Because I'm Craig Campbell's woman and—"

"Ah, yes," Linn interrupted and began to dry-wash his hands, the action as gleeful as his expression and tone of voice. "I was sure I heard you correctly when you were pleading for Mr. Edge to spare you. He was not moved by your appeal, but you saw that I and my fellow thespians were impressed."

Edge lit his cigarette and rose from the tree root. He moved slowly, for the sake of his bruised body, but Maguire was suspicious and made to bring up his Spencer carbine.

"If you aim it at me, kill me," Edge rasped. "Try to give folks the one warning. They don't take heed, I do my best to kill them. Fact that I'm still around shows I ain't never managed less than my best."

The tone of his voice and the glint in his eye was sufficient to make the short and stocky Maguire hold still and listen. But when Edge was through, the Spencer began to move again. But it came to a halt when Oliver Strange called shrilly, "Don't, Henry!"

He allowed the barrel to droop and the scowl became a sneer as he watched the half-breed go slowly and with obvious pain toward the center of the track where Fay Lynch still sat, her legs splayed under the full skirts of her modestly high-necked dress. "Just for you, Olly," Maguire rasped. "But these damn tough-talking cowboys

76

get my frigging goat! It's my belief they talk more bullshit than they ever step in!"

There were only two words which were capable of arousing the killer instinct within Edge these days. In the past there had been many and in days gone by Henry Maguire's tone of voice might have been sufficient to rile the half-breed. But on this cool early morning in the greenish light of the mountain forest, the man had not called him a Mex or a greaser. So there was no change in the attitude of the tall, lean, dark-skinned man as he stooped—causing Fay Lynch to draw back from him with a gasp—and picked up the Frontier Colt which had belonged to a man now dead.

The good-looking blond-haired boy had begun to sweat and now shifted to the side so that he could keep the Winchester aimed at the seated woman after Edge stepped into his line of fire.

"Ain't a cowboy, feller," Edge said as he began to eject the spent shellcases from the chambers of the Colt, letting them fall into the pine needles between his feet. Then he glanced at the cowering woman. "Nor a gunslinger, lady. But it doesn't bother me getting called either. Does bother me when I get robbed and when people shoot at me."

He returned to the tree root and disappeared from sight into the timber. He went in the direction he had seen the mare lunge when Fay Lynch and the two gunmen advanced on her. He had reloaded the Colt with the shells in his shirt pocket and two from the loops of the gunbelt by the time he found the mare, grazing contentedly on a patch of lush turf. He was still within earshot of voices at the start of the track. But he made no effort to decipher what was being said.

With the Colt in his holster and the Winchester back in the boot, he drank some canteen water and splashed some on his sweat-tacky face, washed the dust off his hands, and then led the mare by the bridle back to the track. The talk had ceased by then and Edge saw why when he emerged from the trees at the top of the shale slope.

Hamilton Linn, a morose frown in place of the smile, stood where the half-breed had last seen him. Hat back on his head and both hands in the pockets of his duster, he was alone except for the two dead men and seemed to be lost in a private world of deep thought from which the sound of Edge's entrance from the timber jerked him with a start.

"I'm going to figure your left hand ain't aiming that little gun at me, feller," Edge said. He continued to grip the bridle of the mare and let his right hand hang free and easy below the level of the Colt butt jutting from the holster.

The elderly actor, who looked even older than he had last night in the livery—and drained and weak now that he was not faking high spirits—shook his head, the expression in his dull eyes not altering. "I'm holding it, Mr. Edge. But not pointing it at you. But I am prepared to try to defend myself against you. If it is necessary. Though I would obviously prefer not to have to do that."

"You plan to try holding the Lynch woman to ransom?"

Linn nodded. "And she would not be any use for that if she were dead, Mr. Edge."

"No sweat, feller." He jerked a thumb at the corpses. "They were the ones tried to kill me."

"On her orders. She said she thought you were a lawman which was why she told the men to shoot you."

"No lasting harm done to me. And they paid for listening to her. You got a better reason for keeping her alive than I have for killing her."

"And you will overlook that I ordered Marybelle to shoot your gun out of your hand, Mr. Edge?" The nervousness was draining out of him and the promise of a smile of relief hovered at the corners of his mouth.

The half-breed dropped his cigarette and ground out its fire under a boot heel. "I didn't like that it happened, feller. But into every life a little rain must fall."

The smile unsteadily lodged itself on the pale face of the elderly actor. And something of the familiar boom returned to his voice as he asked, "And you do not attach any blame to me for the accident of you being knocked out by the drunken liveryman two nights ago?"

Edge had swung up astride the mare as Hamilton Linn asked this. Now he shook his head slowly from side to side, a head that if it still ached did not cause great discomfort—or no more than all the other areas of pain over his torso and limbs. From the vantage point on his horse, he grimaced down the long, steep slope at the end of the ravine. And growled, "Seems I've been getting rained on a hell of a lot these past couple of days."

Hamilton Linn was on the point of becoming anxious again. But then he realized the half-breed was simply thinking aloud. "You'll return to Ridgeville with us, Mr. Edge? We are camped just a half-mile or so to the north. We'll start back just as soon as we have had breakfast."

"A half-mile away?" Now Edge was brought out of a period of private reflection—and the actor's anxiety increased when the glittering blue eyes fixed him with an untrusting stare. "How come you happened by this way in time to—"

"It was most fortuitous, that is all," Linn hastened to explain, and the smile was back, full of his happiness at being able to supply such a ready explanation. "We made camp very late last night, totally unaware that there were others in this area. This morning, before we could light our own fire, we saw the smoke of another. And we came to investigate, Mr. Edge. Reached the campsite of the Lynch woman and the two men just as they were preparing to leave.

"Of course, we had no idea who she was at that time. Then, lo and behold, everybody heard you coming up out of the ravine. Although, again, we had no idea it was you. If we had, we would have intervened earlier." He shrugged. "But we did not realize until later that this was any of our business. A point of view which you fully understand?"

Edge arched his eyebrows. "Sure, feller."

"You will return with us to Ridgeville?"

"No, feller. I still have business out here in the mountains."

Linn was puzzled. "But surely . . ." he began, then thought he saw the light. "Ah, you received a commission to recover the stolen money, Mr. Edge? Of the kind I proposed to offer you before the drunken James hit you with the bottle? And you will not be able to earn your reward unless you personally—"

"That ain't it, feller," the half-breed interrupted. "Like I said awhile back, I don't like to be robbed. And I was robbed while I was out cold in the livery the other night."

"Oh, dear," Linn said softly, and gulped.

"Seems the liveryman is the prime suspect."

"And he left town claiming he intended to avenge the murder of the sheriff."

"You got it, feller."

"But if that is what he truly intended, he would hardly have stolen your money, Mr. Edge. And if he did steal your money, he will be far from here by now."

"Where?"

"I beg your pardon?"

"Where would JJ be if he stole my money?"

Hamilton Linn shrugged his shoulders and shook his head, eyeing the half-breed with a puzzled frown. "I can hardly be expected to know that." Now he nodded. "Nor can anybody else who does not know the man well."

"And the only friend he had got shot dead in the bank raid. I'm just like anybody else, feller."

Linn nodded wisely this time. "So you are uninterested in the Campbells as such? Except as a magnet drawing the man James? And if you find him, you will then need to look elsewhere for the thief?"

"In which case I'll see you back in town, later," Edge answered and touched the brim of his hat as he heeled the mare forward.

"Me? Why me? Surely the fact that I came out

here and risked my life to recover our money is proof that—"

"Easy, feller," Edge cut in evenly on the unusually shrill voice of the elderly actor. "Didn't mean anything personal. Just a manner of speaking." He saw a smile of relief spread across Linn's face, then turned to gaze over the corpses of John and Arnie to the natural track between the trees.

"Break a leg, Mr. Edge!" Even as he called this after the half-breed, Hamilton Linn realized it would probably be misunderstood. So he hastened to add, "It's a theatrical expression! A manner in which we thespians convey good wishes for a performance!"

Edge continued to ride on by the dead bodies and did not turn in the saddle as he murmured, "Won't bother to say obliged, feller. Way bad manners are on the increase."

Chapter Eight

FAY Lynch and her two hapless escorts had been camped at a spot where the track turned to run due west. Edge picked it up in this direction and remained astride the mare, rolling and lighting a cigarette, as he surveyed the site. A pile of ashes with a few embers still glowing: the morning fire whose smoke the Linn Players had spotted. Droppings and signs to show where three horses had been hobbled during the night. And three elongated indentations in the soft ground—two on one side of the fire and one on the other—to reveal where the trio had slept in their bedrolls.

The three had struck camp, which required no more than to douse the glowing ashes of the fire, when they were disturbed by the sounds of the half-breed's approach. They had gone to check who was coming—unaware that they were themselves under surveillance by six members of the Linn Players company of actors.

By the time he had smoked half the cigarette, Edge had seen enough to visualize the actions and reactions of the Lynch woman and her escorts and to corroborate Hamilton Linn's account

83

of what happened. He needed to do this because he was not prepared to accept the coincidence at face value.

Then, convinced that the elderly actor and his troupe were on the level, his thoughts turned to the lesser coincidence of his run-in with three members of the Campbell bunch, who had to know the country between here and Cloud Pass better than a stranger. Before John and Arnie made the mistake that got them killed, it was clear that they were escorting the woman back to Craig Campbell. And after Edge dismounted and squatted down on his haunches, his slitted eyes spotted the necessary clues amid pine needles that showed that the three riders had reached the campside from the southeast. He also saw older signs leading away from the other side of the trampled area.

These caused a wintry smile to flit across the thickly bristled features of Edge as he dropped his cigarette butt on the fire ashes, kicked dirt over the red glow, and then gingerly mounted the mare. For they meant that the spot where the track swerved from northwest to due west and where the three travelers had made their camp was on well-used route through the forest on the valley side.

He was quietly satisfied with the result of his brief investigation and confident that he would be able to follow this regular trail which members of the Campbell bunch apparently used to journey between their bolt-hole at the pass and the outside world. Hence he would not need to do any more backtracking and could be sure that in making detours to the left or right he was still on the right path.

Because of the thick foliage of the towering trees, the atmosphere on the floor of the forest remained cool and damp throughout the long morning as the lone rider moved slowly through the timber. Across spongy ground that was constantly sloping upward. The light was always green and a little misty, stray shafts of warm sunshine occasionally locating a patch of dampness to vaporize.

Perhaps thirty minutes after Edge and Hamilton Linn parted company, the creatures of the forest grew accustomed to the presence of the half-breed astride the mare and began to go about their daily business with the same sounds and pace as usual. The birds and animals ceased to fear the quiet intruder who progressed without haste but with resolute determination toward an objective that was none of their concern. And, of course, because it is the way of nature, it so happened that some creatures that ignored the lone rider were intent upon killing other inhabitants of the forest.

But this parallel did not occur to Edge as he pressed steadily toward Cloud Pass. For he did not have that kind of philosophical streak in his character. He was simply aware of the calls and the cries and the scurries and the scratchings as audible signs that all was well. And listened to them in the knowledge that an abrupt cessation of the chorus could well signal that he was no longer the only human intruder in this section of timber.

The muted barrage of sound continued unabated throughout the morning and into afternoon while the rider allowed his mount to make the pace. The sun had moved more than halfway down the south-western dome of the almost obscured sky before he called a rest and meal halt. He did so at the crest of a rise on the valley slope from which he could see for the first time today the twin peaks which flanked Cloud Pass. He saw, too, that in locating the way by which the Campbell bunch moved to and from their headquarters, he had considerably cut down on the traveling time the giant of a lumberman had said it would take. He guessed he could reach the eastern start of Cloud Pass in less than three hours without going any faster than before.

When he looked back down the valley slope he could see several columns and smudges of smoke against the mostly pine-green backdrop of the far side of the valley. He picked out two as coming from the stacks of the company sawmill. North of these, there was a layer which he guessed was composed of smoke from many chimneys in Ridgeville—it was thick enough to blot out the sheer face of Indian Bluff behind the town. Elsewhere, the scattered lumber camps were marked by the smoke which rose from heaps of burning tree trimmings.

The creek could not be seen, nor the town, nor the lumber-company installations. Just the many smoke signs that there were people in the dense forest below.

Edge sat on a small knoll and ate a cold meal of stale biscuits and hard cheese washed down with canteen water. Smoked a cigarette and waited for another fire to be lit—his back to the valley bottom so that he could watch the wooded gap between the twin peaks, which was about a mile wide at the bases of the ridges.

After almost two hours, when the northeasterly pointing shadows had grown long and the air had chilled enough for him to don his sheepskin coat, he saw the smoke of the suppertime fire of which Fred Caxton at the timber company sawmill office had spoken. It rose from a point a little left of center about midway through the pass.

Edge mounted the mare and followed the well-trodden way until twilight and then full night clamped down over the mountains. He had gone half the distance between the knoll and the fire in the pass. Then he swung down from the saddle and led the horse by the reins, angling away from the direct route to the camp to head for the base of the ridge to the south. He did not go all the way to the moonlight-reflecting rock, though. Instead he halted and hitched the mare to a low-hanging branch, slid the Winchester out of the boot, and followed his nose—having begun this final leg of his approach when he was close enough to smell the smoke of the fire in the cold night air. The acrid scent of burning wood was mixed with a faint aroma of coffee. There was no longer any smell of food, for that had been cooked and eaten during the time it had taken Edge to get this close.

Since darkness had fallen, the sounds of the forest had changed as the nocturnal creatures came out into the open. They did not run and skulk at his passing since they were familiar with having man as a neighbor in the pass—man in the sense of mankind, since they were also familiar with women. Indeed it was a woman who shrieked with laughter no more than forty feet

87

from Edge, who abruptly froze in mid-stride, hands fisting tighter around the frame and barrel of the Winchester.

Then came a guffaw from a man.

"Quit it!"

"What's so damn funny?"

These two men sounded irritable and both seemed to get what they wanted. For the sounds of good humor were curtailed and a man said something in low tones that Edge was unable to hear. Whatever it was, it struck nobody else as humorous and silence descended again.

Edge backed up to a tree and dropped to his haunches, resting against the trunk, the rifle laid across his thighs. The faint smell of coffee made his mouth water and he swallowed the saliva rather than spitting it out.

From time to time there were short, soft-spoken exchanges. Between men, among women, between men and women. Perfunctory and desultory on most occasions. He could tell this from the tones of their voices and the intervals between the snatches of talk. As if the unseen group—he could not guess at how many were in it—was waiting for something to happen. Were already bored from a very long wait and expecting it to be some time yet before it was over.

Edge himself waited with stoic patience. Moving very little in order to keep his muscles from stiffening up and only to blow warm breath into the cupped palms of his hands. Puzzled by the situation beyond the timber ahead of him, but not willing to move blindly toward a group of people obviously prepared for a long-awaited and not welcome event. He certainly was not it, but in the dark night which would suddenly be taut with high tension, it would probably not be safe even for the mother of any man or woman at the camp to show herself much less a stranger.

His elbows and kneecaps smarted from where they had been skinned in his slide down and climb up the shale slope of the ravine. But there was no ache in his head anymore. And he felt only slightly abrasive skin on his temple where the bottle had been smashed. He could recall being in worse shape than this on many other occasions.

He had been just as flat broke, too.

But, with a scowl that involuntarily drew back the thin lips from his teeth, he could not remember ever following such a long-shot lead to get something he needed.

"Shit, this is friggin' crazy!" a man snarled. "That sonofabitch ain't out there no more, Craig!"

A rifle shot cracked. It seemed to come from a long way to the right of where Edge suddenly straightened against the tree, thumbing back the hammer of his own Winchester. But this was an illusion created by the echo effect in Cloud Pass, for the gun had been fired within effective range of the impatient man who had just spoken. The man—or somebody close by him—cursed and then groaned.

"The bastard got Roy, Craig!" a woman announced in a tone of awe. "Right through his heart, goddammit!"

"Serves the big-mouthed dimwit right!" came the rasping reply. "Anybody see anything?"

"Frig it, no!"

"Wasn't expectin' nothin."

"He's to the north, that's for sure."

"Maybe Ewan and the boys got a line on him this time."

Edge had been closing the distance on the group, taking short and probing strides, testing the ground for dry twigs before he set his foot down fully. But now he froze again, at the whispered relevation that some of the Campbell bunch were out stalking the timber of the pass, hunting the riffleman who had apparently struck before. The grin which had replaced the scowl on the face of the half-breed faded as he considered this danger that he did not know had existed until now.

"Don't count on it. Whoever it is out there, he's smart. I just hope that the two men fetching Fay are smart enough not to come riding in here large as life if they've heard that shot."

Edge moved forward again, under cover of the rasping, anxious-toned voice of the man he assumed to be Craig Campbell. Grinning quietly again. For two reasons now.

Firstly, he was too close to the camp to be in danger from the men hunting the timber; he had run that risk without knowing anything about it. Secondly, John James was alive and well and doing exactly what he had told the people back at Ridgeville he intended to do.

Which meant that JJ, who was the only citizen of the town he had any respect or liking for, was not a thief. Which maybe Edge had never considered him to be from the outset. Which in turn maybe meant that he had known that every yard he traveled away from Ridgeville put him that much farther away from his bankroll and the thief he intended to kill. But it also got him closer to where he would be able to lend JJ a hand. Even if JJ had not asked for help—JJ being the kind who never asked for help.

Edge knew that kind very well.

He was about to step around a double-trunked tree when another shot exploded in the north section of the pass. It was the less powerful crack of a revolver. And no bullet thudded to rest in the area where Craig Campbell and the others were waiting.

"Hey, you think that was—"

"Shut up," a man snarled at a suddenly excited woman.

Edge jerked back behind the double trunk.

From the area where the revolver shot had sounded, a man bellowed, "We got him, Craig! And you ain't never gonna guess who it is!"

"I ain't in no mood for guessing-games, Ewan!" the second Campbell brother roared. "Not with three dead boys down here!"

Ewan sounded at the peak of excitement. Craig was in a trough of dark rage.

"Okay, we're bringing him down!" Ewan called and now he sounded sullen.

"Hope the bastard is still alive," a woman rasped. There were some grunts of agreement with this.

"Where the hell is Fay and them two boys who were supposed to fetch her?" Craig Campbell snapped.

Ever since the news had been shouted that the man with the deadly rifle had been captured, the previously tense group at the camp began to relax. Matches were struck and tobacco smoke was now drifting through the trees and mixing with the pine scent that filled the half-breed's nostrils. Then he smelled wood smoke and saw a flickering light as the ashes of a fire were stirred into life and fresh fuel was added to crackle and spit sparks. Next he saw a steadier light—the yellow glow of more than one kerosene lamp. And all the time, the group was dispersing over what seemed to be a large area—an intriguing fact which Edge did not move forward to investigate until Ewan Campbell shouted, "See, you people! Look at who it is, will you? Old drunk JJ from the livery at Ridgeville! What do you think of that?"

This drew some low-toned responses and Edge heard the voices but not the words as he stepped out from behind the double trunk and crossed the final few yards to reach his objective.

As he did this, the rasp of many voices was curtailed by the shrillness of one.

"Damn you to hell, you Campbell sonsofbitches! Damn you for killin' my best buddy! And for gettin' me before I made you pay!"

"Sittin' up on a rock outcrop large as life and twice as ugly. Drunk and crazy both, I figure." Ewan spoke with venomous scorn.

And his brother answered with the same brand of contempt—but directed at Ewan and all who agreed with him. "Why's it always me has to do the friggin' thinkin' around here? A man that's drunk and crazy don't shoot good as that!"

Edge was in a position to see what was happening now. He was in a fringe of trees that encircled what had once been an army fort, built with the timber that was felled to make the initial clearing for the fort. Fire had ravaged the place a long time ago so that now there was just a single building left standing amid the charred and weed-covered ruins of others and the stockade wall that had surrounded all of them.

Lamplight shafted from the four glassless windows and open doorway of the long and low building that had probably been a barrack in the former fort. And additional illumination was provided by the cooking fire in the center of the onetime drill square.

The glow of the moon was barred from this area of the pass by the ridge to the south. In the artificial light, Edge saw more than a score of men and women in two groups. Craig Campbell was at the front of one group, and as he spoke he gestured with a wave of a hand toward a line of three corpses on the ground at one end of the building. He did so as the last one to die was briefly displayed, then draped with a blanket like the other two.

Ewan Campbell stood a little apart from the second group which was comprised of just himself and five other members of the Campbell bunch—two of them flanking the defiantly scowling John James and holding him by the upper arms and wrists.

The successful search party had come over the weed-choked base of the former stockade wall and into the fringe of lamp and firelight before they stopped to show their prisoner to an audience of a half-dozen women and twice as many men. An audience that viewed the short and rotund figure of the Ridgeville liveryman with a mixture of emotions—varying from hatred to anger, and curiosity to indifference.

93

But nobody looked elsewhere after Craig Campbell's gesture. And JJ himself divided his scowling attention between the Campbells. Thus the woman who had covered the corpse of the man named Roy was unseen as she crossed herself, kneeling on the ground, and ran the back of a hand across both her eyes to wipe away the tears.

Craig Campbell asked, a little absently, "What are you ramblin' on about JJ?" Then a thought occurred to him and he took a step toward the prisoner and snarled, "You do any fancy sharphshootin' before you got here?"

"I'm talkin' about you people shootin' down Bart Bolt when you hit the Trasks' bank, that's what!"

"What's he . . ."

"I said did you use your rifle . . ."

A man behind Craig Campbell started to pose the first question. Then Campbell interrupted and a gunshot interrupted Campbell. It was fired from a revolver in the double-handed grip of the weeping woman who had covered the corpse of Roy. From the dead man's gun, which she slid from his holster as she rose from her knees and turned to stare and aim at JJ.

The bullet took the liveryman in the chest, high and to the right, and he grunted with surprise and looked down at the blossoming stain on his jacket. He felt the pain and sagged, but he was held up on his feet by the men who flanked him.

Every head wrenched around to locate the person who had fired the bullet. Everyone saw the woman with the tear-stained, anguish-contorted face as she staggered toward JJ, thumbing back the hammer.

"You killed my Boy, you rotten old man! You shot him down like a dog, you coward! From out there where nobody could—"

"Aw, shit!" Craig Campbell snarled, and shot the woman in the side of the head at point-blank range.

Edge, dropping to his haunches behind a screen of low-growing brush, murmured, "Something smells worse than that about this, feller."

Chapter Nine

THE killing was a totally cold-blooded one.

Like every other man within the confines of the derelict army post, Craig Campbell was dressed western style. Hats varied in shape and color; and coats, shirts, pants, and spurred boots likewise; some outfits well-fitting and others too large or too small. But every man carried a revolver in a way best suited to him.

Craig Campbell drew his army Colt from a hip holster on the left side of his gunbelt. Without undue speed, but with a certain deliberation that did not extend to slowness. Then he brought it swiftly to the aim and squeezed the trigger. This while the woman grieving for Roy was still closing with the sagging JJ, too intent upon abusing him and finishing him off to be aware of anything else.

When the .45-caliber bullet smashed into her head she pulled up short and became rigid, dead on her feet for part of a second. Then she dropped her man's gun and collapsed limply to the ground, an area of darkness rapidly spreading in her blond hair.

It was as if she were forgotten the moment after

she was dead. And no one moved to align her with the other three corpses. All attention was directed at her killer as he holstered the Colt and stepped forward, motioning for the still-conscious JJ to be lowered to the ground.

This was done and the Campbell brothers hunkered down to either side of the softly cursing liveryman. Nobody else closed in on the three of them. Some backed off a pace or so, as if made nervous by the brutal killing of the distraught woman.

"You sayin' the Ridgeville bank was hit, JJ?" Craig Campbell asked.

"You friggin' know it, you—"

The back of Craig's hand cracked hard against one of JJ's flabby cheeks. "I ain't talkin' because I like the sound of my own voice, stupid!"

"Nor yours!" Ewan snarled, like a man eager to show he was as hard as another.

From his secret vantage point, the now impassive half-breed could see the Campbell brothers were big men. As big as any lumberman back in Ridgeville—except for the giant named George— but he could make out little else about them. At the distance from which he watched the harsh interrogation, figures were no more than dark forms on the fringe of the fire and lamplight.

"And you friggin' killed Bart Bolt and the Trasks!" JJ countered. His head wrenched to the side with the blow, but he refused to cry out in pain. "You or some of this crud you run with up here!"

"Crud, are we!" Ewan roared, and brought back an arm to throw a punch into JJ's fearless face.

97

Craig said, "Quit it, Ewan," in an even voice and it was sufficient to cause his brother to halt the move. Then he drew his Colt again. The click of its hammer had the impact of thunder in the stillness of the army post. Everyone present momentarily froze, as if under a spell. Then a burning log on the fire cracked and the spell was broken.

And Craig said coldly, "You're known as a talker, JJ. And that's what I'm tellin' you to do. Tell it plain and simple, what brought you up here to gun for me and my brother. Do that now, JJ. In the same way as usual. Or do it later, like a girl."

"Soprano," a man among the watchers growled.

"Yeah, soprano," Craig echoed, and thrust the muzzle of his gun harder into the groin of the liveryman.

And John James did as he was ordered. But not because he was afraid of being emasculated by a bullet from Craig Campbell's Colt. For there was no quiver of terror in his voice, weak thought it was from the effect of the bullet in his chest. Yet he spoke in somewhat of a puzzled tone at first, and later in a tone of misery. This tone was heard after he'd told of the bank raid and triple murder at Ridgeville. "I frigged it up, ain't I" he said bitterly. "You kept your word? It wasn't you Campbells nor any of your bunch?"

"You're damn right it wasn't," Craig answered in a rasping tone. Now at last he drew a gasp of pain from the wounded man as he thrust the Colt harder into his crotch. "Now tell me what I asked awhile back? You see anybody while you was comin' up to the pass?"

"Just them crazy theatricals in their wagon, Craig. But they won't ever get that heavy rig—"

"Theatricals?"

"Yeah. Bunch of folks come to town to put on shows for the people there. Seems they'd deposited their money in the Trasks' bank. Bill Sheldon, he said he'd bring cash from Casper to replace what was took of the lumbermen's pay. But them theatricals weren't gonna get any of that. So they figured to come up here and . . ."

JJ had become eager to please now. He was talking fast, leaving no pauses. As if he considered he would be safe for as long as he kept Craig Campbell interested in what he had to say, and did not allow the importunate brother to question him further.

But the man with the revolver in his fist had heard enough. And he made this known by squeezing the trigger of the Colt.

The resulting shot was muffled because the muzzle blast was partially absorbed by the inverted vee of JJ's thighs. The shock of the second bullet tearing into the flesh either killed or drove the liveryman into instant unconsciousness. And he uttered no sound as his body shook with a single violent spasm.

Craig was on his feet by then, the revolver back in his hip holster. As he turned to survey the bulk of his audience—along with his brother—Edge saw their faces for the first time. Ruggedly good-looking faces, alike enough to be twins, although only Craig sported a narrow mustache. Lean faces with prominent cheekbones, the flesh darkened by sun and wind and the eyes and teeth showing up brightly in the lamp and firelight. He guessed they were in their early thirties.

"Okay," Craig said coldly. Ewan watched him speak, continually altering his expression and the set of his eyes to try to copy the look of his brother. "Nobody owes nobody anythin' around here. So I'm askin' a favor. As many of you as are willin' to help me find my woman?"

He raked his eyes over the faces of the men and women in front of him, his body and limbs in a lazy attitude designed to convey the fact that he was ready to cope with any response he drew. His brother's attempt to imitate this stance was child-like.

"If they got her in that town down there, Craig?" a man asked.

"Then that's where we go, Leo."

"And we don't leave until we had our fill?" another man asked.

"What d'you think?" Ewan put in before his brother could reply—and his tone of voice was as bombastic as his stance was swaggering.

"Terrific, Craig."

"Let's get movin'."

"The women, too?"

"That'll be like takin' snow to Alaska, dammit!"

"Shut your mouth, Daniel Grover!"

"Yeah, we wanna have a little fun, too."

There was a great deal of argument, all of it good-humored, as the bulk of the crowd moved away from the unmoving spread-eagled form of John James.

Ewan grinned triumphantly at the success of Craig's call for help, while Craig frowned as he watched the crowd disperse, some going into the fort's one remaining building, most heading for the forest. "Go get our horses, Ewan," Craig instructed.

Ewan moved to comply with the order, and his grin became a scowl as he raked his gaze over the three men and one woman who remained. When they ignored him, he spat in the fire to show how he felt about this.

"What happened to Roy, that was just dumb bad luck," one of the three men said dully, and touched the toe of a booted foot to the corpse of the dead woman. "But you didn't have to do that to Dotty, Craig. You could've knocked the crazy dame down. Or shot her some place that didn't kill her."

"I could've sure enough," Craig allowed. Without the slightest trace of emotion in his voice or his expression.

"They were with us, Roy and Dotty," another of the three men said. "We were together a long time, dammit."

"So?" Ewan countered in a rasping tone.

"So it ain't right!" the woman came back shrilly. "We come up here to this asshole of a place because the law and bounty hunters was gunning for us. And what friggin' happens? It ain't safe like it's supposed to be. It ain't no safer than—"

"Today's been exceptional," Craig cut in.

"What?" the woman snapped.

"Ain't no one never dared to come in here shootin'," Ewan answered and gave his calm and quiet brother a nervous sidelong look. "That what you mean, Craig?"

"Quit it, Ewan," Craig said evenly. He slightly

altered his posture so that he squarely faced Roy and Dotty's four friends, his gun hand hanging close to the butt of the Colt in the hip holster. As an afterthought, he spread a grim scowl cross his face, then asked, "You want to do more about this than gripe?"

At his secret vantage place, Edge vented a low grunt and smiled, pleased that Craig Campbell's stand suited his own ends and feeling a sneaking admiration for the man.

Ewan was pleased, too, his face lit up with a broad grin of anticipated pleasure as he adopted a gunfighter's stance alongside his brother. People began to appear from around the rear of the building leading saddled horses by the bridle or reins. The initial surprise on their faces changed to curiosity or eagerness or, in a few instances, a brand of impatient boredom.

"Hell, we're just sayin' it don't seem right that we—"

"Jesus Christ, you yellow bellies!" the woman cut in on the apologetic man. "What we're sayin' is that this asshole of a place ain't worth one stinkin' cent of the big money we paid. And you guys gotta do somethin' about it! If not for us, goddammit, then for Dotty and Roy!" She moved her head from one side to the other, glaring scornfully at all three of her male companions in turn.

"What you want us to do?" the apologetic man asked of her. As he spoke, the man who had brought the subject up to begin with went for his holstered gun.

In this situation Ewan did not need to defer to Craig. He knew exactly what to do and was able to do it a fraction of a second faster than his brother.

Both were quick-draw specialists, but neither sacrificed accuracy for speed. Ewan shot the man who was first to go for his gun and Craig blasted a bullet into the man who moved instinctively to respond—stopping him before his revolver was halfway out of the holster. Two heart shots across a range of perhaps ten feet, the impact of the lead in the chests thrusting the men toward the left before they crumpled to the ground.

The woman carried no gun, but she was not unarmed. As she vented a high-pitched scream and lunged toward the brothers she brought her right hand away from her waist fisted around the handle of a knife. Her left was curled into a claw, the long nails aimed at the grinning face of Ewan Campbell.

The brothers saw that the surviving male member of the disgruntled quartet was frozen by shock, and therefore no danger to them for the moment. So both raked their Colts an inch or so to the side and fired simultaneously—when the point of the knife was no more than a foot away from Craig's throat and the talon-like hand had come almost as close to the gleefully shining eyes of Ewan.

Heart shots again, the two .45-caliber bullets tore through her body from such short range that they stopped her in her tracks. She stood tautly erect for a moment. Then she toppled backward like a felled tree, her arms raised in the attitude of attack until she was halfway to the ground. Then she went limp and hit the ground flat on her back. This jolt caused gouts of crimson to spurt from the two holes below the mound of her left breast.

"You?" Craig asked of the no longer rigid man who was flanked by the corpses of his companions and looked to be on the verge of collapsing with terror as he stared down at the woman with the massive bloodstain on her shirt.

The man jerked his head up to look at the two brothers. His entire body seemed to move like a marionette with the strings tangled. If the Campbells had taken the time to notice the expression of pathetic helplessness on the man's face, they would have realized there was no aggressive intent in the way his hands traveled toward his gunbelt.

But they were the kind of gunfighters who judged a situation by deeds rather than moods. And again, before the smoke from their last double killing had dissipated in the night air of the derelict fort, they squeezed their triggers in unison.

The victim screamed, "No!" And started to stretch his arms into the air as a sign that he did not intend what the Campbells thought. But it was too late and the monosyllabic denial completed itself as a croaking groan of despair. He took one backward step, dropped his head forward to look down at the bloody holes left of center in his chest, then fell to his knees and went into a sprawl on his belly.

No one reacted to these killings. They remained either curious or eager or bored while they waited for what was to happen next.

"Like I said," Craig growled as he began to extract the spent shellcases from his revolver. "Go get our horses."

104

"Sure thing." Ewan again had to check what expression his brother was wearing, and adopt it himself, before he could swagger away to do as he was told.

Craig reloaded the Colt and pushed it back into his hip holster before he addressed the quietly waiting group. "Never happened before and I intend to see it never happens again. The trouble with the crazy liveryman from Ridgeville, I mean. With this bunch . . ." He waved a hand to encompass the three men and two women he and Ewan had gunned down. ". . . and their kind of trouble, it never got to be this much of a problem before. But it can always happen again."

"Sure, Craig," said a redheaded man with bushy side whiskers whose name was Leo. "Wasn't nobody's fault but their own."

"That's right," another man agreed. "They knew the setup here. Same as all of us. And they heard what JJ said about the bank raid and killin's in Ridgeville."

"You don't have to prove nothin' to us."

"I never liked them high-nosed Texans."

"Some Texans is all right, Brodie."

While the eager and the curious contributed to a babble of talk, Craig Campbell briefly smiled his satisfaction that the recent slaughter had not undermined his authority over the fugitives at Cloud Pass. Then he went into the remaining building to fetch out two saddles. The others got their gear and prepared their mounts for riding.

Not until Ewan came around a corner of the building leading two horses by the reins did a woman ask: "Shouldn't we do somethin' with the dead?"

She addressed the question to anybody who was prepared to answer it and when everybody was astride his or her horse, all looked at the Campbell brother who was apparently better at everything except the fast draw.

And Craig Campbell replied coldly, "It's a woman that better still be alive concerns me. The dead will keep. Maybe until we've had our fill of Ridgeville. Maybe forever."

This drew a cheer from some throats.

Then Craig jerked on his reins, Ewan did likewise, and the Campbell brothers headed their mounts toward the distant town in the valley bottom. The rest of the men and women went after them, the mood of all becoming varying degrees of tense anticipation—from the anxiety that Craig was feeling and his brother was trying to ape to the evil relish in Leo's grin.

Then the whole group was gone from sight, and within perhaps two minutes, the sounds of the riders through the timber faded from earshot. At this moment, his voice competing only with the crackle of the dying fire, the painfully wounded liveryman from Ridgeville spat out in an embittered tone, "You've gone and done it wrong again, JJ, you crazy old fool." He spoke as he eased gingerly up into a sitting position and raked his scowling gaze over the draped and uncovered corpses. "And when you make a mistake, you sure make a bad one, feller," Edge said as he advanced out of the timber into the aea of the fire and lamps.

"Uh, what's that? Who's that?" The liveryman turned his round face with the bushy gray mustache and the tiny eyes toward the half-breed.

106

He did not recognize him until the tall, lean figure towered immediately over him. "Well, I'll be. The stranger. What are you doin' up here at the pass? You one of them like some folks reckoned you was?"

Edge dropped down to his haunches and briefly eyed the bullet wounds. The one in the upper right chest of JJ had not bled very much and perhaps was not serious. But the whole crotch area of his pants and the ground beneath was deeply stained by spilled blood. There was no color in the man's cheeks and his eyes looked to be blurred with tears. His grimace showed that he was struggling not to reveal how much pain he felt in his shattered genitals.

"Came to ask you one important question, JJ."

The wounded man had to spread both palms out on the ground behind him to keep from sprawling out on his back again. "It could be I'll only have time to answer the one, mister."

"Did you steal my money before you came up here?"

The grimace on the fleshy, wan face abruptly changed to a scowl. And JJ tried to spit a globule of saliva at Edge. But he did not have the strength and it just dribbled out of his mouth, ran down his jaw, and dripped onto his shirt. "Pretty damn easy to call a dyin' man names, ain't it? I ain't never stole nothin' from nobody in my whole life, mister."

"Obliged," Edge said and rose to his feet.

"Hell, mister, don't leave me alone to die!" JJ pleaded, as the half-breed made to turn away from him.

"It's what you'd do if I didn't come up here to

the pass to insult you," Edge pointed out. And continued his move away from the twice-wounded man.

"Hell if I'd let any of them know I wasn't dead, they'd have finished me."

"So you wouldn't have died alone," came the reply as Edge stepped through the open doorway of the last structure left standing within the former army post.

It had been a barrack in the old military days and required little alteration to serve a similar purpose for civilians of both sexes. Long and narrow, it had a row of beds down either wall, with one end curtained off by blankets hung from the rafters. It could accommodate twenty people sleeping one to a bed, but there was ample room for others on the floor. Most of the people staying here had cleared out all their personal possessions for the ride to town, but here and there on the shelves above some beds were photographs, brushes and combs, and an occasional bottle of liquor—invariably opened.

Edge grabbed the fullest bottle of rye and went back outside. JJ was still holding himself in a sitting posture, waiting intently for the half-breed to emerge from the building. He expressed relief when he saw him, and then managed to raise a grin of pleasure as he saw the bottle Edge was carrying. "Is that what I think it is?"

Edge glanced at the label as he went down on to his haunches in front of JJ again. "It ain't the best, feller, but then I guess in your state of health, the best would be wasted on you."

"In my state of health, even the worst there is would likely taste like the best I ever had." He made to lift a hand and reach for the bottle, but then realized he would topple over. Disappointment clouded his small eyes and pulled his mouth into a strangely childlike set.

"Take it easy, feller," Edge told him, and took the stopper from the bottle. He reached forward and tilted the bottle, then said, as the wounded man opened his mouth and drank greedily, "Was looking for money to pay you for allowing me and my horse to stay in your livery, JJ, when I found out I'd been robbed. You'll accept this liquor as payment in kind?"

The liveryman was still drinking, and he got the peevish expression back on his face when the neck of the bottle was withdrawn from his lips.

"You hear what I said to you?"

"Sure."

"We have a deal?"

"Sure."

Edge allowed him to drink again and watched for a signal that he should pause. But no sign came, and the near three-quarters full bottle of rotgut liquor was emptied with just the one unwelcome interruption.

The half-breed tossed the bottle away and took the makings from a shirt pocket. He remained close to JJ and leaned the Winchester against his leg as he rolled the cigarette.

"Any more where that came from, mister?" the no longer wan-faced man seated on the ground asked.

"Some."

"I'd sure appreciate it if you'd go bring me some more, mister."

Edge struck a match on the butt of his holstered Colt and lit the cigarette, replying on a stream of smoke, "I don't steal for myself, feller. So I sure don't do it for other—"

"You didn't have no money to pay me, so you didn't have none to buy that liquor you just give me." Now he was even talking as well as pouting like a spoiled child denied what has been demanded.

"Robbed Peter to pay Paul. Figure to find Peter down in town and square things with him."

JJ gave a throaty sound of disgust, looked long and hard up at Edge, decided the calmly smoking man was not going to be quickly persuaded, and so gingerly lowered himself down to his back again. By the time he achieved this, his face was beaded with sweat and some fresh moisture had broken through the crusting of old blood on his wounds. But John James had not cried out in pain. He simply sighed his relief when he was sprawled out on the ground in relative comfort after the agony of moving had subsided. Then he said, "You're a strange one and no mistake, mister. Maybe there's time left for me to straighten you out."

"Strange but not queer, JJ," Edge reminded him evenly with the hint of a cold smile drawing back his lips and narrowing his eyes to the merest slivers of glittering blueness. "And I just told you I'm not a thief."

"You ain't makin' no sense, mister." ,

"Just that in no sense do I need to be straightened out on account of being bent."

110

Chapter Ten

"GUESS that's some kinda joke you just made, mister," JJ said through teeth clenched against the pain that it was getting harder for him to endure. "I ain't in any mood for them, though."

"I won't make any more then," Edge told him evenly. "So what should we do while we wait for you to die?"

"You're some kinda hard bastard!" the wounded man accused, then sighed and added, "yet in some ways you ain't. You're really gonna do like I asked and stay with me, ain't you?"

"No sweat."

"Why?"

"Maybe because a night's board and lodging for me and my horse is worth more than a few swallows of cheap whiskey."

"Balls!" JJ came back sneeringly, then winced and reached with both hands toward the injury at his crotch. But he stopped short and smiled briefly and without mirth. "Bad things for me to say."

"Yeah, a sore point, JJ."

"That's gonna be the death of me." Now the light of good humor shone in his small eyes. But only for a moment. "There has to be somethin' more to it than you made out, mister. On account of you're smarter than that."

"Smarter than what, JJ?"

"You knew that if I'd took your money, I wouldn't come gunnin' for the Campbell bunch. And if I come for them, I wouldn't take your money."

He gazed up intently at the tall half-breed with a cigarette angled from the side of his mouth and the Winchester canted to his left shoulder, tacitly pleading to be told the truth.

"What do you want me to tell you, feller?" Edge asked flatly.

John James made a low whistling sound and shook his head slowly from side to side twice. Then in an even, unstrained tone, he said, "You know, mister, you're a lot like the kinda man comes to Cloud Pass. Reason you got cold-shouldered by a lot of folks down in Ridgeville."

"No more than you," Edge pointed out.

"Reckon not, mister. And when I look back on how I was when I first come to town, I can see how I was like the kinda man who comes up here. Changed some, I guess. With time. Don't set out to work so hard at bein' different from other folks. Just do what I wanna do and to hell with what them other folks think. You ain't no spring chicken no more, mister. Near about time you stopped actin' so mean when you ain't really feelin' that way. And pretendin' you're doin' things good for the wrong reasons."

"Like the hard men who come up to the pass when the going gets too hot other places, JJ?"

The man on the ground grimaced. "I guess a guy like you gets around, mister. Guess you've met all kinds. Good and bad. But I doubt you ever come across a meaner bunch than some of them that hide out here. And none meaner than Craig and Ewan themselves. Outlaws every one of them. Wanted all over for every crime you can think of—and some you can't, maybe."

Edge smoked his cigarette, mind as blank as the expression on his lean, heavy-bristled features, while the fire died and its light and warmth receded from the night.

"Craig and Ewan worked for the company a year or so ago. Highballin' high climbers the both of them. And if you don't know the loggin' business, that means they were real fast at their job and they was the kind that went to the tops of the trees when high-lead loggin' was needed. Real risky to do." He grimaced, but this was due to present pain rather than bad memories. "Though lumber-jackin' was their business, they had other irons in the fire. Couple of territorial marshals from Arizona showed up in town one day. With warrants for the arrest of the Campbells. Charge of murder and rape.

"Good old Bart, he went out with the two Arizona lawmen to bring in the Campbells from where they was workin' over to the other side of Indian Bluff. But Craig and Ewan, they must've seen them comin' and guessed what was up. Went for them with broadaxs. Just cracked good old Bart over the head. But when they was through with the Arizona guys, there wasn't hardly any-

thin' left of them that was recognizable human."
JJ was getting weaker and a new look showed on
his face—fear. It could only be the fear of what lay
beyond the threshold of beckoning death.

Edge tossed the butt of his cigarette onto the
dying fire that might or might not outlive the man
and dropped to his haunches again. "If you figure
another bottle will help, I guess I can run to—"

'No, mister," JJ cut in. "Reckon I've drunk
more than my fair share and maybe it'll go better
for me if I ain't drunk when I get to the big roll
call." His voice was not so strong now and he
talked faster, anxious to get said what he wanted
to say. He frowned, the wan and flabby flesh of
his face creasing as he strained to recall where he
had left off.

Then: "That was the start of good old Bart's ru-
ination. Him wakin' up to find them Arizona guys
spread all over the place with what looked like
more blood spilled than rain falls in a winter. And
the Campbells hog-tied by a bunch of Ridgeville
loggers who'd heard the rumpus and come runnin'. But he got the brothers back to town and
locked in the cell of the law office. Then wrote a
letter down to Arizona for somebody to come get
them."

JJ was gazing straight up at the starry sky. He
rolled his eyes without moving his head to look at
Edge and asked, "You like me well enough to roll
me a cigarette, mister?"

"No sweat."

"Small enough thing after all the trouble you
been to on my account, huh?" Another small
smile, showing a great deal of strain this time.

"I'll keep my hat on, feller."

114

"Huh?"

Edge had taken out the makings and was already rolling the tobacco in the paper. "So as the light from my halo won't get in your eyes."

JJ bared his teeth in a grimace of pain. "I'd have to be a real fool to call you a saint, mister."

"And a fool you sure ain't, JJ," Edge answered, completing the cigarette, lighting it, and offering it to the dying man.

"You'll have to take care of it for me, mister. It's like I'm paralyzed." He tried two draws of the cigarette, then coughed violently, cursing between the spasms that triggered fresh pain from his bullet wounds. Fresh blood oozed out and spread over the caked blood. When the coughing fit was over, he growled, "Guess I'll give up smokin' as well as drinkin'."

"And all the women left, JJ," Edge told him, then hung the cigarette to one side of his own mouth.

"I give them up a long time ago, mister. Though it's gonna be one of my deathbed regrets that I never got to screw that prim and proper Emma Roche that keeps the boardin'house. Seen if I could've proved my belief that all she needs to make her human is only what a man can give her. Though I ain't a man no more, am I?"

"Guess no life is ever long enough to do everything somebody wants, JJ," Edge muttered, as tears that were not caused by physical pain glistened in the small eyes of John James.

"Frig it, I'm wanderin' and it ain't because I'm drunk. Appreciate it if you don't sidetrack me no more, mister. On account of I want to get this told." His moisture-sheened eyes directed a ques-

115

tioning look at Edge, who remained impassive. "Hell, I can see myself in you just like it was yesterday. When the only thing I was scared of doin' was showin' my emotions."

"You've been down that sidetrack and I didn't say a thing, feller."

"Shit!" He returned his gaze to the night sky, and after perhaps three seconds of concentrated thought, he was able to recall the point at which he had broken off to request the cigarette. "Yeah, I remember. Couple of months after good old Bart wrote the letter, three guys showed up claimin' to be lawmen. But they didn't look like that was what they was. And they had a woman apiece who wouldn't've looked out of place in a two-dollar-a-trick whorehouse.

"Me, I never reckoned good old Bart was took in by them guys. Said from the start he handed over the Campbells to keep them from startin' bad trouble in town. Others, they reckoned he was yellow. Or plain dumb. That he could've done somethin' to stop them Arizona lawman gettin' hacked to pieces. And he let the Campbells outa jail because he was too scared to put up a fight. That, or he couldn't see the guys that come for them wasn't lawman like they claimed.

"Hell, mister, good old Bart was the law in a lot of tough towns down south before he came to Ridgeville to retire."

"He didn't die young."

"Sure enough didn't. I reckon he was way past my age. A lot older than sixty. And all this I'm tellin' you, it happened only a little over a year ago. But he was a proud old guy and not suited to retirement. Just kinda appointed himself sheriff because Ridgeville didn't have no lawman. Not that it ever needed one until the Campbells came and brought trouble along with them.

"But that ain't here nor there. I'm of the opinion that there was nothing good old Bart could do when the killin's happened over to the other side of Indian Bluff. And that he done what he did in the interest of Ridgeville folks when he turned the Campbells over to them other three hard men and their women." JJ directed a tacit challenge up at Edge, who continued to sit on his haunches and merely turned slightly to send his cigarette butt into the ashes of the fire.

"I wasn't there, so I can't know, one way or the other, JJ," he said.

"Nor friggin' care!" came the snarling response. "Because good old Bart wasn't your only friend! And you'll be movin' on pretty soon! Not givin' a damn that he'll be buried in a town where everyone but me thinks he was a crazy old man who . . . Aw, dammit, I'm sidetrackin' myself again, ain't I?"

"Yeah."

The dying liveryman squeezed his eyes tightly shut and snapped them open again. A look of melancholy spread across the mask of pain that had gripped his features several minutes ago. "The stars ain't any dimmer to you, are they?"

Edge glanced skywards and answered, "No, JJ."

"I can smell death."

"Not your own, feller," the half-breed told him and wrinkled his flared nostrils as he looked around at the neat line of blanket-draped corpses

117

and the sprawling, uncovered bodies. "Craig Campbell was wrong. The dead don't keep."

"Whatever, I'm gonna be one of them pretty soon."

"You been saying that for a long time now, JJ."

"Shit, you want me to say I'm sorry for takin' so long about it? Okay, I'm sorry I held you up!" He was still strong enough to be angry.

"You didn't, JJ. Somebody else did. For the best part of a thousand dollars."

"So go find out who it was and get your money back, mister," he invited, no longer enraged, his tone almost sly. Then: "But you ain't ready to, are you? You're too interested in what I'm tellin' you?"

"Yeah, JJ," Edge answered. He knew it would not be long now, he could tell from the man's abrupt change of attitude that he was not feeling pain anymore. That merciful numbness had come to the bullet-shattered areas of his body and that with the paralysis which gripped JJ's nervous system had come a euphoric sense of well-being—a feeling that was the very opposite of his true condition. "You tell me about it, JJ. Ridgeville people say you're a real good talker."

"Ridgeville people!" the liveryman muttered and the smile that had started was abruptly clouded over with bitterness. "Who gives a shit about them? Let me tell you about Ridgeville people, mister."

And he did. About the derelict fort at Cloud Pass, too. And about how he had come up the side of the valley in a state of extreme drunkenness. How he was doing a fine job of killing those he felt sure were responsible for the death of his

118

only friend—until Ewan Campbell and the other men jumped him. He explained how it was he'd been able to do this so expertly.

Occasionally he moved away from fact, and from conjecture based upon fact, and began to ramble off into the realm of wishful thinking. About how it was all right he had killed the wrong people. Because Ridgeville people were just as guilty and soon they would get what was coming to them. Some of them, at least, when the Campbell bunch hit town.

He couldn't recall why they would hit town and asked Edge to prompt him. And the half-breed reminded him about Craig Campbell's suspicion that his woman had been captured by Hamilton Linn and his troupe of traveling players.

"Oh yeah. Them folks is all right, mister. I didn't take to the old feller when he said somethin' bad about good old Bart. But I can understand him now. He didn't know my good buddy. And he was all steamed up about gettin' robbed. Like you, mister. But you said . . ." JJ was adrift in a hazy limbo and had just a fingerhold on reality. But he bore down for a while and sought to tighten his grip.

"Yeah, you said you wasn't gonna help him. So he went ahead and helped himself. Him and his buddies. And me. Now you. I took a swing at him with a bottle. Hit you. You didn't come up here to the pass because I hit you with the bottle, did you?"

Edge shook his head.

JJ said, "What, I didn't hear you?"

Edge opened his mouth to reply, but then realized the man would not hear him even if he shouted at the top of his voice. For he had slipped out of his waking limbo into a state of coma.

The fire was out by then, but John James still had a couple of hours of life left to live. He spent them on a bed in the barrack-like building while Edge nearby, listening to the shallow breathing and alert for any change that might signal the fact that JJ was on the verge of coming out of it. But he did not. There came a time, while it was still dark outside the lamplit building, when the man breathed out and did not breathe in again.

Edge was smoking when this happened, and as he swung his feet to the floor he dropped what was left of the cigarette under one of his heels. Then took one of the blankets off the bed where he had been resting and draped it over the newest corpse at Cloud Pass. Before he allowed the fabric to fall over the waxy-looking face, he murmured, "After drinking, smoking, and women, JJ, breathing was about all you had left to give up."

Chapter Eleven

EDGE went back to where he had left the mare and brought her up to the abandoned fort. He unsaddled her and put her into the rope corral behind the barrack to feed and drink while he went inside the building and doused the lamps. He lay down in the curtained-off section, far removed from the bed on which the blanket-draped corpse of John James was beginning to stiffen.

He chose to separate himself from the dead body not because it was dead—he was too familiar with death to be morbidly concerned by its physical presence. He did so out of respect for the man who had once occupied the body under the blanket—on the premise that there is no dignity in death and the least he could do for JJ now was to allow him privacy as he began to return to the dust from whence he came.

Or he could have buried him, Edge reflected as he came to the brink of sleep—fully dressed and with his hat over his face and his left hand fisted around the frame of the Winchester—but the thought was fleeting. He needed to rest for what little was left of the night, and even when the new day broke, he knew he would not bother to put JJ in the ground. They had never been that close.

Not close at all, of course, Edge thought as he washed up and shaved before a mirror-topped bureau in the section of the barrack where women guests of the Campbell brothers were able to maintain some semblance of modesty. Sunshine began to burn off the dawn mist and draw the night chillness out of the air.

They had been alike, that was all—except that JJ was more than ten years older than Edge. That short a time! He finished scraping all but the bristles of the Mexican-style mustache off his face, washed off the soap, and leaned closer to the cracked and mottled mirror.

The lines inscribed in the dark-hued skin were many and deep. But how many were of relatively recent origin and had much had they deepened in the last few years? He could not tell, because he had not looked at himself this closely before.

Now he finger-combed his hair and brushed some loose strands off his shoulders. This was nothing new, had been happening for some time now. But this was the first morning he had been moved to peer closely at the loose hairs on the dark-colored fabric of his shirt—to see if any were gray. None were.

Which was small consolation as he hefted his gear and carried it out of the segregated section of the building, down the aisle between the beds in the area where the corpse of JJ was beginning to smell, and into the sun-bright open air. Where the stink of death was much stronger but was almost totally masked by the fragrance of pine forest at morning.

Did his saddle and bedroll and accoutrements seem to weight heavier? Did it require a greater degree of effort to swing the saddle and gear across the back of the mare? Was the crick in his back when he unbent after buckling the cinch and the creak in his leg joints as he got astride the horse in his imagination, or was each a very real symptom of the physical decay which accompanies the passing years? The inescapable aging process which comes to all men, no matter how unlike most others they consider themselves to be?

Edge heeled his mount out of the corral, around the side of the barrack, across the former compound with its scattering of stinking dead, and onto the easy-to-follow trail left by the large group of horsemen and women who went down from the pass in the night. He spat twice and then lit the cigarette he had carefully rolled—all the while watching to see if his hands showed the slightest tremble.

By the time some smoke had been drawn into and expelled from his system, the sour taste of too many yesterdays had been removed from his mouth. But his mind remained uneasy until he forced himself to consider what JJ had told him last night.

What JJ had told Edge could have been said in a fraction of the time it had actually taken. And the half-breed endeavored to get it down to the basic facts in his mind, without wandering off the way the dying man had rambled away from the subject.

After Craig and Ewan Campbell had been released by the elderly sheriff, Bart Bolt, into the custody of the trio of obviously phony lawmen, the town of Ridgeville had returned to normalcy. The only difference was that the self-appointed town peace officer was treated with even more scorn. Which he accepted with tacit indifference and continued to go through the motions of being the lawman in a town where nobody broke the law.

Bolt's only friend was JJ and as the liveryman was always quick to point out, the feeling was mutual. The two men, one a good deal older than the other but alike in many other respects, spent a good deal of time together. Swapping stories of the past. Bolt telling yarns about his days running the law offices in many Texas towns while JJ told about fighting Indians before the war and fighting Yankees during it.

From time to time, when the circumstances had seemed right, JJ had tried to pump Bolt for information about the release of the Campbell brothers. But the elderly sheriff had always maintained that the three men who came for Craig and Ewan were genuine territorial marshals who were traveling with their wives.

Until the day that two more men rode into Ridgeville—some three months after the Campbells left town—and showed papers which proved undisputably that *they* were Arizona marshals. And announced that they had come to check on the whereabouts of the men who had been buried as two heaps of chopped meat in the Ridgeville cemetery.

Bolt had started to plead ignorance of the

whole affair, but the townspeople were quick to point out that he was lying. Which was when the Campbells and the first of their constantly changing 'bunch' rode onto Pine Street and gunned down the Arizona lawmen. Then Craig told Bart Bolt he was a crazy old fool for not telling the people of Ridgeville of the deal they had struck that day three months earlier. When the elderly sheriff could have blasted both Campbells into eternity—but would have been gunned down himself by the fake lawmen, and would have died with the knowledge that this trio and their whores would then put the town to the torch and kill as many women, children, and old people as they could before the loggers came running to the rescue.

Alternatively, Bolt could have put up the gun with which he was covering the Campbells. And in return for this, many lives in addition to his own would be spared. And the town would be protected for all time—or, at least, for as long as Craig and Ewan maintained a hideout for fugitives at the derelict fort up in Cloud Pass.

Sheriff Bart Bolt had accepted the deal and thus had compromised himself as a lawman. And had been ashamed of himself, irrespective of the fact that making the compromise had secured far more than his own continued existence.

For a while, after Harry Bellinger had buried two more out-of-town peace officers in the Ridgeville cemetery, the citizens had treated Bolt as a hero—maybe overreacting to their earlier contempt. But now the boot was on the other foot and Bolt spurned their attempts to fete him, remaining scornfully aloof to everyone except his

125

old friend John James. And, as the smoke of the cooking fires in Cloud Pass was seen for what it truly was—instead of being assumed to mark the camp of some trappers or hunters—every deep-thinking citizens of Ridgeville experienced the same brand of shame which twisted in the belly and guts of Bart Bolt.

But this period passed by and time had its healing effect on the consciences of the loggers and the merchants. Sometimes the Campbells came to town; at other times strangers appeared who made it known that they were heading to or from Cloud Pass. Hard men all of them, often with painted women who wore revealing dresses and swayed their hips more than was necessary.

Bart Bolt knew many of them from the years he'd served as a peace officer in other towns. But those that he did not know were poured from the same mold—a man didn't have to be a well-traveled sheriff to see that.

But they stopped at Ridgeville only to buy supplies, to take a drink or two in the saloon, eat a meal, have a haircut or bed down for a night or more in greater comfort than the trail or the derelict fort at the pass offered. There was never any trouble and none of these visitors—with their gunbelts slung around their waists and their smiles that never put light into their eyes—ever took anything he did not pay a fair price for.

Twice, lawmen had come up from the south and twice they left convinced that the Campbell brothers had never been there—and that the four Arizona marshals who preceded them had ridden out of town after receiving the same answers to the same questions.

Occasionally, when loggers were working in areas far from Ridgeville, stories were recounted of gunfire heard far off to the south or southwest. The townspeople realized that men were probably getting killed. Lawmen and bounty hunters trailing the fugitives who sought refuge at the sanctuary run by Craig and Ewan Campbell. Men who had gotten too close to their quarry or been spotted by lookouts posted by the men already holed up at the pass.

But the matter was seldom pursued for very long. Because such talk always ended up torturing the townspeople with doubt and guilt and shame. Law-abiding people who condoned the lawless deeds of the shifting population of their neighboring community up the hill. And why did they do this? To have the protection of the killers and robbers and kidnappers and rapists. Which meant protection from the protectors—for until the Campbells brought that kind of trouble to Ridgeville, it had never come before. Ridgeville was just too far off the main trails through the Rocky Mountains to attract such people.

Only two citizens of the lumber town ever considered putting matters right. Bart Bolt and John James. The two men who talked and drank for hours at a time in the sheriff's office or the livery stable. The sheriff always remaining sober enough to keep his friend from going off half-cocked to implement one of the endless impossible plans of campaign they dreamed up.

Such was the situation when Edge rode into the outwardly serene and untroubled town of Ridgeville just four days ago. And had been assumed by all to be on his way into or out of Cloud Pass.

Disliked at sight but accepted once he showed he was not here to make trouble.

Then came the bank robbery and killings and after the initial shock had passed, the ostriches of town shoved their heads back into the sand. Not believing that any group from Cloud Pass was responsible and hopeful that the Campbell bunch would take action against the raiders. Confident of a fresh supply of money from the company—not enough to make good what was stolen, but sufficient to keep them safely in the Ridgeville area while others took risks and maybe got lucky.

The town drunk.

A group of no-account actors.

And a lone stranger who on first impression might just have been involved in the bank raid but who was later given the benefit of the doubt.

The Linn Players and this man named Edge were not local citizens and so the town could not be blamed for whatever actions they took against the Campbell bunch. While everybody knew that John James was a great friend of Bart Bolt and a drunk.

What nobody in Ridgeville or Cloud Pass knew about JJ except for the late sheriff was that he had once been an Indian fighter and an expert marksman with a rifle. He had developed both skills while he was in the army, long before he took to the bottle, and both were recalled and used to reasonable effect when he reached the pass. After he had taken the time to sober up from the long drunk that the death of good old Bart had provoked.

In the old days, JJ had ruefully told Edge as he neared death, he would have killed more of those sonsofbitches. Maybe every last one of them. From a distance and with the sniping rifle. And some up close with a knife. The way he had killed so many stinking Indians and frigging Yankees and lived to tell the tale. Then he had asked Edge to remind him why the Campbell bunch were riding for Ridgeville.

And now, as the half-breed reminded himself of his own reason for returning to town, he shook his mind free of memories from a more recent past. And discovered he did not need to work at barring unwelcome thoughts from his head.

For a distant fusillade of gunshots captured his attention, driving home the unspoken tenet that he had always lived by: that a man who walked the thin line between life and death was only as good as the next step he took. Now, as he got a bearing on the direction of the shooting beyond the thick-growing timber to the east, he was able to smile again. Maybe the younger fellers walked that line faster, but that kind were easier to trip up.

He kept the mare to the same easy pace on the downslope while the gunfire continued to sound, sporadically after the initial violent burst, for perhaps a full minute. Then it ceased abruptly and the forest silence enclosed this section of the valley again—disturbed only by the soft clop of the mare's hooves until other living creatures in and under the trees decided it was safe to go about their business again.

The man who could be said to be both in and under a tree was not a living creature. He was hanging with a rope around his neck from a very

129

high branch of a Douglas fir, his booted feet suspended some thirty feet above the ground.

Edge saw him the moment he rode into a glade. But as he reined the mare to a halt and gazed up at the hanged man, he guessed that the Campbells and their bunch had passed directly under the dangling feet, in the darkness of night without being aware of what was above them. Thus they had not read the message that was written in large letters on a piece of white board and tied with string to both wrists of the dead man:

> HE FIGURED HE WAS A BIG MAN LIKE
> YOU CAMPBELL. BUT WHEN I WAS
> THROUGH WITH HIM LOOK WHAT HAPPENED.
> AL FALCON.

The man who hung as still as the death that had claimed him was the Montana Lumber Company's top man in Ridgeville—Bill Sheldon.

Edge set his mare moving again and touched the brim of his hat as he rode under the dangling corpse with the bloated face and a bad smell. He glanced briefly up at Sheldon and muttered, "For somebody in the timber business, feller, you sure finished up close to the top of the tree."

Chapter Twelve

IT was getting close to noon when Edge found the corpse of Bill Sheldon and read the message that explained so much about recent events—even to a man who was on the outside looking in.

In no great hurry to find out anything more about this business, which was really none of his concern, the half-breed stopped for regular meal breaks, bedded down from dusk until dawn, and did not get back to Ridgeville until eight o'clock the next morning. He heard no more shots fired in all this time; in fact, he heard no sounds that was not a sound indigenous to the forest for virtually the whole way to Ridgeville. Which was not as it should have been on a work day in the vicinity of a lumber company.

Thus he rode with more caution than usual as he neared town and altered his intended line of approach when he arrived at a lumber camp. It was deserted but not abandoned—with tools scattered around, sap still oozing from the stumps of recently felled trees, and some red embers among the ashes of yesterday's bonfire. He veered south of the route the Campbell bunch had taken and within thirty minutes emerged on the trail close to where he left it three days ago. He had to ride no more than a thousand yards around a sharp curve to reach the sawmill.

It looked to be in the same forsaken condition as the lumber camp. The buildings were silent, the bandsaws idle, the chimneys not belching smoke and the smell of escaped steam absent. Wagons and trucks were haphazardly parked, some partially loaded or unloaded with cut timber and logs, their teams gone from the traces.

Edge looked and listened hard, his left hand holding the reins loosely while his right lay deceptively relaxed on his thigh, a few inches from where the stock of the Winchester jutted from the forward-hung boot.

There were no signs of violence here either. Both the camp and the sawmill had simply been deserted by the lumbermen at the end of yesterday's work. And, Edge reflected as he heeled the mare forward and angled her across the yard of the mill, both places doubtless looked like this every Sunday morning. And on public holidays. But on such occasions there would not be a sense of evil clinging to the atmosphere and seeming to cast a pall over areas that should have been vibrant with activity and noise.

Edge sensed it—almost smelt it—but was not affected by it. Ever since he had left Cloud Pass to return to Ridgeville, he had known there was a better than even chance that deadly danger was waiting at journey's end. He was almost at the end of the ride now and it was only to be expected that he should feel the tension start to build as what he suspected began to be confirmed. But he

132

could take no more precaution than he was already doing, so he remained as impassive and as apparently relaxed as before.

At the bank of the creek at the north end of the sawmill's main building he swung out of the saddle and allowed the horse to drink from the fast-flowing water which sparkled with warm morning sunlight. Then he led the mare by the bridle toward Ridgeville, staying as close to the creek as the timber and brush allowed. Not trying to mask the sounds of his progress but poised to draw the Colt from his holster if he was heard and challenged. Leading the horse with his left hand on the bridle, walking to the right of the mare so that the booted rifle was easily accessible. In the event that somebody up on the heights of Indian Bluff made the mistake of taking a shot at the half-breed, missing, and then showing himself.

For Edge was in a killing mood.

"What on earth are you doing back here, Mr. Edge?" Fred Caxton asked in a nervous tone.

If the half-breed had not instantly recognized the voice of the lanky young man with sandy hair and ink-stained fingers who was the timber company clerk at the sawmill, it was likely Caxton would have died before he finished the query. Likely or even certain, Edge thought as he forced himself to untense after the effort of staying the move to draw the Colt. He halted and froze to stare at a ten-foot-high clump of brush ahead and slightly to his left. "Still looking for the money that was stolen from me, feller."

Caxton made a lot of noise trying to break through the brush to get to where Edge stood with his horse on the bank of the creek. But not enough to keep the half-breed from catching a sound from another direction.

"Stay there and I'll come out to you. Shit, damn thorns! Mr. Edge, have things been happening since you left! Ouch! The people of this town are finally making a stand . . . Oh, sweet Jesus, no . . . !"

There had been a rustling noise in another area of brush. Edge backed along the side of his horse and slid the Winchester from the boot. The sounds were made by one or maybe two men closing furtively with Fred Caxton and the half-breed. The excited youngster had not heard them because he was making too much noise himself. But suddenly he saw them. Before Edge could get an accurate bearing on the source of the danger beyond the green and brown wall of brush and tree trunks.

Two of them. One blasting revolver shots at the suddenly terrified young man who was trapped in the tangle of thorny brush. The second firing blindly with a handgun in the general direction of Edge. Firing so fast he had to be fanning his revolver.

The mare was hit and snorted as she pivoted on her hind legs and tossed her head in the air. Her right hindquarter slammed in the chest of Edge and sent him staggering backward, a curse ripping from his clenched teeth. The killer urge threatened to expand the ice-cold ball of anger from the pit of his stomach to his entire being. He could feel it turning white hot.

But then he lost his footing and toppled onto his back. He knew he was going to splash down into the creek. And he also knew at the moment of impact, as the water sprayed up about him, that the mare had probably saved his life. For a second revolver was spitting out potential death at his falling form as the man who had taken care of the hapless Fred Caxton joined the attack on Edge.

The half-breed sucked in a deep breath and dived. But his head was under the surface for only a second or so since the creek here was shallow. Drowning was not a danger here, but being trapped by the tacky silt on the bed was. If his moves were slowed by the grasping mud, the two men would have the time to reload their empty guns. Or maybe plunge out of the brush with rifles ready to pour bullets into another hapless victim.

The mare was down on her side, flailing all four legs. Her coat lathered with sweat as she tried to reach the closest of two bloody wounds in her flank with her bared teeth.

Edge caught just a glimpse of this and fought the hot rage it sparked as he turned to the side and used his heels in the silt to propel himself upstream. He had to reach the nearest cover, a rotting log imbedded in the creek bank. Once there, he turned again and rolled over onto his belly just as the two men burst into sight. One held a rifle and one a revolver, its loading gate snapping closed as he emerged on to the creek bank near the suffering mare.

Edge had to expose himself above the log to get clear shots at the two men. The one with the rifle saw him immediately. "Shit, we only plugged his horse," he growled. Very fast.

Fast enough to have uttered the whole sentence

before Edge squeezed the trigger of his Winchester and drilled a bullet into his heart. The man stared at him in horror and frantically tried to rake his Winchester to the aim.

The man with the revolver wrenched his gaze from the struggling horse, his expression altering from anger to terror. He started to search for the falling form of his partner, but realized it was more important to locate the half-breed. But in the time it took for his change of mind to communicate itself to his muscles and for them to respond, Edge had worked the lever action of his repeater, shifted the aim of the rifle, and squeezed the trigger.

A belly shot this time, because this was the first area of the new target to present itself. The man was knocked backward.

"Sonofabitch!" he said, then brought up his revolver and tracked it toward Edge. Squeezed the trigger.

Edge hurled himself onto his back again, working the action of the rifle. His lips draw back from his teeth as another curse rasped out.

The bullet smacked into the rotten wood of the log and spattered slimy pieces of it in all directions.

"Sonofabitch!" the man said again.

Edge raised himself to a sitting posture in the running water of the creek, the cocked Winchester aimed from his shoulder. He saw the man on the bank holding his revolver in both hands and struggling hard to thumb back the hammer. But his coordination was gone and he could not manage the simple task.

He looked up from the Colt and at Edge seated

136

in the water. He giggled and said, "I bet it's cold in there."

"Enough to give an old man rheumatics," Edge told him. And shot him. Aiming for and hitting the man in the throat, the bullet entering his flesh on a rising trajectory. From close enough range to have the velocity to explode into the open again just below the crown of his head. The mess of gore that sprayed from the bullet's exit inscribed an ugly stain across the creek bank.

From a distance came the shouts of men, then the crackle of gunfire. To the north and the west, in and to one side of Ridgeville.

No bullets rustled through the brush or impacted with the trees in the area of the creek bank where three men were dead and one rose and struggled out of the clinging mud and fast-moving water.

Edge made no assumptions. He merely continued to watch and listen. His field of vision was very limited on three sides, but extended far up and down the creek and to the top of the bluff.

But the bluff was totally clear. It appeared that the townspeople had posted just the one sentry on the bank to the south of Ridgeville and just two of the Campbell bunch had come to cover the same area.

The shooting subsided after the initial volley to a desultory exchange. This lasted until Edge was out of the water and squatting beside the now quiet and unmoving mare. Water dripped from his sodden clothing as he lay his rifle on the ground and examined the two wounds in the flesh of the horse, then explored them with his fingers. She had been hit in the withers, just ahead of the saddle's front jockey, and in the thigh. She had bled profusely but was not bleeding now. Nor was she still in great pain, as could be inferred from the way the animal lay trustingly calm.

He guessed that since they were revolver shots, fired over a range of several feet, they had not drilled into the mare very deeply. And he knew there were no vital organs in direct line with the wounds.

"If you can get up and make it as far as town, I figure you can pull through. Long as there's a vet in Ridgeville."

He fisted a hand around the rifle and stood up. The mare vented a low snort and eyed him wistfully. "Up to you, horse," he said. "You've carried me a lot of miles. But I can't return the favor, even as far as town. And that has nothing to do with me not being so young as I used to be."

The mare snorted louder, made a nodding motion with her head, and tried to rise. She failed with a sigh that quivered through her whole body and caused fresh blood to trickle from the bullet holes.

Edge stooped and gripped her bridle. He tried to offer encouragement. "You can do it."

He tugged gently and for long moments thought the animal's spirit was broken. But suddenly the mare flailed all her legs, rocked from side to side, and lifted her head. Edge had to move fast to get clear of her, but he maintained his hold on the bridle. Seconds later she was on her hind legs and foreknees. It seemed that every tendon in her body was bulging and that she did not possess that final ounce of strength necessary to get herself four-footed.

Edge cursed at her through clenched teeth, but held on to the bridle and resisted the temptation to tug, for fear it might upset her delicate balance as she gathered herself for a final effort. Then the set of his lips changed from a grimace to a grin and a terse laugh burst out of his throat as the mare delved deep into her reserves and pushed herself fully upright.

"Easy," he said soothingly and stroked her neck for a few moments while she looked like she might collapse. But this weakness passed and she was sure-footed again. Weak from shock and loss of blood but willing to go on.

"Least I can carry the freight," he muttered, and uncinched the saddle. When he had it and his bedroll slung over one shoulder and the rifle canted to the other, he grinned again as he surveyed the horse, the two dead men on the bank, and the bullet-riddled corpse of Fred Caxton slumped but held partially erect within the tangle of brush. "Surprising what we can do when we have to, horse," he said lightly and felt too good to let the smile fade as the discomfort of water-logged clothes began to make itself clammily apparent. "In your case when you're shot. And in mine when I only thought I was."

Chapter Thirteen

HAVING found out the hard way that the creek was shallow close to its west bank, Edge utilized the knowledge and waded back into the water. With both hands full, he could do no more than cluck to the mare and beckon with his head for her to follow him as he started upstream.

And the horse followed, maybe relishing the feel of the cold mountain water that came no higher than her knees but perhaps communicated its coolness to every part of her pain and fear-heated body.

Edge was only vaguely aware of the temperature of the water as he trudged against the current and set his feet down carefully to test for any sudden change of depth. All the while he continued his watching and listening surveillance over his immediate and more distant surroundings. The horse kept pace with him, blood dripping steadily from both wounds momentarily staining the water of the creek and being quickly eddied away.

For perhaps five hundred feet man and animal waded around the curving water course and Edge

knew they had to be getting close to town. At any moment he expected to see the rear of the JJ Livery Stables at the southeastern end of Pine Street.

But it was a group of men who showed themselves in the timber on the creek bank before he was close enough to Ridgeville to see any of its frame buildings. Rifle and ax-toting men who were as much a part of the town as its buildings.

Drawing close to the silent and grim-faced group, Edge recognized the tall and thin Doc Hunter, the redheaded Moss Tracy, who ran the town saloon, and two of the lumbermen who had come to the assistance of Fred Caxton at the sawmill the day he left to go to Cloud Pass. One of these was Quinn, who had been prepared to gun down Edge with the half-breed's own rifle. He was armed with just a broadax now, which he held across his chest with both hands as he glowered at the newcomer more grimly than any of the other five men.

"You get to kill the kid this time, stranger?" Quinn asked and stepped forward, brandishing the ax as Edge made to come out of the creek and up on to the bank.

"Get out of my way, feller," Edge answered.

"Quinn, let the man out of the water first," the Ridgeville doctor instructed in a tone that lacked authority and sounded a little afraid.

"I still ain't so sure this guy ain't with the Campbells," Quinn growled, and glanced at the rest of the group as if seeking signals that some of them agreed with him.

Then he froze, except for his head, which turned slowly and tilted so that he could look down at Edge again, no longer grim-faced. His attention recaptured by the half-breed, who had swung the Winchester away from his shoulder to rest the muzzle lightly against the lumberman's denim-contoured crotch.

Edge did not thumb back the hammer until the fear-filled eyes of Quinn had shifted from the rifle to his face. Then he said, "If you don't follow the doctor's orders, feller, you're going to end up a very sick man. Or something that used to be a man."

"Do like he says, Quinn," Moss Tracy snapped impatiently. "If he's a wrong one, what can he do alone against the whole friggin' town?"

The lumberman expressed a tacit question with his eyes and Edge acknowledged this with a nod. And the moment Quinn backed off, the half-breed shouldered the Winchester, tossed his gear onto the bank, and extended his free hand. Quinn took it, and when Edge found a foothold in the bank, heaved to help him out of the creek.

"Obliged," Edge told the again scowling lumberman. "Caxton's dead. Shot by a couple of men from the pass when he got over excited at seeing me and gave away his position to them."

Most of the men snapped their heads around to peer downstream as Edge rested the rifle against his saddle and began to coax the mare to the bank.

"What happened to them?" somebody asked.

"I killed them. They shot my horse."

"Didn't friggin' matter they killed Fred Caxton," Quinn growled.

"The kid acted like a fool," Edge answered, and

142

managed to get a hold on the mare's bridle. "My horse was just doing like I told her."

"Caxton was doing what he volunteered for, Edge!" Hunter snarled. "The same as we all are! And who knows how many others were killed in the shooting that started because you—"

Edge seemed not to be listening to the embittered doctor as he murmured soft words of encouragement to the weak mare and tugged gently on her bridle. Then Hunter was forced to curtail what he was saying as Edge yelled at the horse and the animal snorted and reared, forehooves beating at the side of the bank while the hind legs thrashed the creek water into white spume.

Quinn hurled down his ax and lunged toward to take hold of the bridle. And it was possible that his strength made the difference between success and failure. The horse came up out of the water and both men released their hold so she could toss and shake her head, pain and weakness momentarily forgotten as she experienced a sense of triumph.

"Obliged to you again, feller," Edge said.

Quinn retrieved his ax and growled: "I got no quarrel with your horse, stranger."

"So you'll tell me if there's a veterinary in Ridgeville?"

"I attend to the ills of animals as well as people," Doc Hunter said with some reluctance. He went over to the horse after thrusting his rifle at Tracy. He looked briefly at the eyes and mouth and a little longer at the still-bleeding bullet wounds.

"This is friggin' crazy!" a lumberman snarled.

"Wastin' time with a sick horse when we oughta be doin' somethin'."

"Doin' what, Groves?" Tracy asked.

"Hell, I don't know. Somethin', that's all."

Hunter backed off from the mare and retrieved his Winchester. "That's a fine animal you got there," he told Edge.

The half-breed had his own rifle canted to one shoulder again and his gear draped over the other. "Can you tell me anything I don't know, feller?"

"The bullets have to be dug out, of course. After that, it'll be a week or two before we can tell if she'll mend good as she was."

"You'll get the bullets out of her?"

"He has more important—" the man eager to be doing something started to say.

"If you'll lend a hand with what's happening in town," Hunter offered.

"Shit, we still can't be sure he ain't one of them!" Quinn complained. "Sneaked in before the time limit to—"

"Goddammit to hell!" Moss Tracy roared, his cheeks almost as red as his hair, his nerves seemingly snapping from tension and suppressed rage. "What the frig have we got to lose by trustin' one man? Time's runnin' out and ain't anybody got any idea what to do when—"

"Okay, okay!" Quinn snarled across the ranting voice of the saloon keeper. "Do what the friggin' hell you want! But if it turns out he's with them, you guys remember what I—"

"Sure, Jack," another lumberman cut in. "We'll have Harry Bellinger carve it on your grave marker. JACK QUINN, THE MAN WHO KNEW IT ALL!"

"If there's any room for him in the cemetery."

"If Bellinger's still around to carve markers and bury people."

The rangy and distinguished-looking Hunter had taken hold of the mare's bridle and started to lead the horse along the bank toward town. Edge followed after glancing at the faces of the five men who were staying behind to guard against an attack on Ridgeville from this direction.

Groves spotted this survey and mistook the lack of expression on the half-breed's lean face for contempt. He snarled to Edge's back, "Well, mister, can you get a two-hundred-fifty-foot-high Douglas fir to fall the exact place you want her to?"

Doc Hunter hurriedly tried placate. "He's nervous, Mr. Edge."

"Scared to death, I'd say," the half-breed answered evenly as he came up alongside the Ridgeville doctor. "And he's got plenty of company. No sweat about what he said, which is every man to his trade. I agree with that."

"What precisely is your trade?" Hunter asked.

Up close to the man and with no need to be concerned with the horse or wary lest somebody get the drop on him, Edge could see he was under as much strain as the rest. When Hunter became aware of this scrutiny, he made an effort to feign composure.

"I supply whatever the market needs when I need to make money, feller. Provided the work doesn't go against my grain."

"The fact that you are back in Ridgeville means you are still in need of money, Mr. Edge?"

"That's right."

"They killed James before you get to the pass? If you got there?"

"I got there, Doc. And they only thought they killed JJ."

Hunter snapped his head around and looked at Edge. There was a glimmer of hope in his weary and frightened eyes. "He's still alive?"

"No."

The hope died and the man looked even more exhausted and afraid in its wake. "But I thought you said . . . ?"

"He hung on long enough to tell me about the situation between Ridgeville people and the hard men at the pass . . . and how it all got started."

"It interested you?"

"No."

They emerged from the trees and entered the yard behind the livery stable. Two men whom Edge recognized as storekeepers were crouched in the cover of a dilapidated buckboard with only one wheel, keeping watch on of Indian Bluff. "What happened, Doc?" one of them called.

"Hey, ain't that guy that . . . ?" asked the other. Neither ventured to expose more than his head above the overturned wagon.

"Fred Caxton was shot dead and Mr. Edge killed the two who did it. So you people take extra care now. It could mean they intend to try to surround us."

"Jesus."

"Why did we ever start this?"

Both lookouts ducked out of sight, but pushed their rifle barrels into view and aimed up at the skyline of the bluff.

Edge and Hunter were vulnerable to a bullet from the bluff and had been so since they left the group guarding the south stretch of the creek. But they felt safe again when they reached the street and headed for the stable.

"So why did you listen to old JJ if you weren't interested?" Hunter asked when they inside.

The livery looked much as it had when Edge left it, except that a few more horses were gone. While Hunter led the mare into a stall, Edge remained on the threshold, lowered his gear to the floor, and gazed out across the street to the forest. He saw no one. But the half-breed could sense many pairs of eyes watching him as he stopped to unfasten one of his saddlebags. And delved for fresh tobacco and papers, having already discovered that the makings he kept in his shirt pocket had been reduced to a soggy mess by the ducking in the creek. Then he rolled a cigarette, conscious of the enmity that was directed at him from several quarters.

"He didn't want to die alone and he stayed a talker to the end," Edge replied after he had struck a match and lit the cigarette. "What time limit, who set it, and when does it run out?"

Hunter came out of the stall after checking the mare over more carefully than he'd done at the creek and halted beside the smoking half-breed on the threshold. "Craig Campbell has given us until noon to accede to his demands, Mr. Edge," the doctor replied, wiping his bloodstained hands on a piece of rag. "Which are to lay down our arms and hand over his woman to him."

"Or else?"

"He has a large force of men with him and they

will attack Ridgeville. Raze it to the ground and kill every last one of us."

"And if you do as he wants?"

"The town will not be touched. And nobody in it will be harmed. Provided they make no objection to the Campbell bunch moving into Ridgeville."

"Moving in for what, Doc?"

"For good, Mr. Edge. Permanently; to turn this town into a much more comfortable version of the old fort at Cloud Pass. For every criminal and outlaw who is able to pay the price the Campbells demand." Hunter sighed and shook his head in misery. "A situation which Sheriff Bolt always said he was afraid might arise. But which nobody ever took seriously. I need to get some instruments and medication from my office, Mr. Edge. Should I stop by the saloon on my way and tell Mr. Linn you are with us?"

"Hamilton Linn's the top dog in this town?" the half-breed asked, surprised.

Hunter sighed again. "It has turned out that way, Mr. Edge. He certainly has some organizing ability. And a manner of issuing instructions which people obey and do not ask themselves why until later."

"Yeah, Doc. You can stop by the saloon and tell him I'm with you." Edge looked up the street to the intersection and shook his head when he saw a familiar figure emerge from the batwinged entrance of the Lone Pine Saloon. "No need. It looks like he's coming to see me."

Hunter glanced in the direction the half-breed was looking and then said quickly and nervously, "Perhaps before you agreed to help, Mr. Edge,

148

you should have known about our problem." He paused, fidgeting. When the half-breed did not fill the pause in with a question, Hunter went on, even faster than before. "You see, Craig Campbell's woman—Fay Lynch—is dead, Mr. Edge. So there is no alternative to a fight. And few of us have the stomach for it. Not because we are cowards or have no pride in ourselves and our town. It's just that we don't think we have a chance of winning against men who make their living with guns."

"Those who live by the gun shall perish by it!" Hamilton Linn boomed as he strode purposefully across the street. "And where there's a will there's a way, is that not so, Mr. Edge?"

"Go get what you need to fix up my horse, Doc," Edge told Hunter. Then, to the actor who abruptly looked less confident when the town doctor strode off: "You're not surprised to see me, feller?"

The slightly built man with the unhealthy complexion hurried into the stable and sagged against the end of the closest stall. He suddenly seemed on the point of collapse as he mopped his brow, licked his lips, and blurted, "Forget surprised, Edge. I can tell you I've never been more pleased to see anybody in my life before. There's a war going to start out there in a couple of hours and I've been elected commander-in-chief of one side.

"All I wanted was our money back. I never planned on something like this happening. We're going to get slaughtered and me and my people will be first in line, Edge. We killed Campbell's woman. She tried to get away and we killed her. We didn't mean to. It was an accident. We fired

149

at her to make her stop and she did. But a rico-
chet hit her.

"But we thought we'd try to bluff it out. That
only Campbell himself or him and his brother
would come. But they've brought a whole army,
Edge. Maybe as many as fifty and ..."

"I'd figure closer to thirty," Edge cut in. "And
some of them women."

Hamilton Linn blinked several times, as if surprised to be interrupted. Then: "Whatever, Edge,
I don't want to be responsible for leading the fight
against them when they attack. But I was elected,
just because I took some of my players after the
bank robbers. And that made the people of this
town feel bad about doing nothing. You went after them, too. And so did the drunk who runs this
place. Dammit, if he had got back here first with
that bunch of outlaws on his trail, he'd have been
elected."

The morning had warmed up considerably since
the half-breed's ducking in the creek, and his
clothes were almost dry on him. But the sweat that
Hamilton Linn was having trouble keeping out of
his eyes and which was mixed in with the spittle
spilling from his quivering lips and trickling down
his weak chin was due only in part to the heat in
the odoriferous stable.

"You feeling any better, feller?" Edge asked as
the actor mopped frantically at his brow.

"Better?"

"For running off at the mouth like a kid scared
of the dark who figures talking will make the
candle light again."

"Dammit it, man, I'm scared all right. But not

of the dark. And I'm nearly exhausted from acting like I'm not to the people hereabouts."

"You looked to be good at your trade when you came down the street just now, Linn."

Despite the circumstances, the man who seemed to look older each time Edge saw him enjoyed the compliment. He pulled himself erect and was less frenetic in mopping at the sweat on his face. "I've been giving the performance of my life, Mr. Edge. As have all the members of the Linn Players. For I am convinced that should we waver in our commitment to stand up against the Campbell brothers and their men, the people of Ridgeville will submit."

"And if they do that, you're dead for killing Fay Lynch."

The actor swallowed hard. "Precisely, Mr. Edge."

"What have you and your people done beside play brave soldiers?"

"The obvious, Mr. Edge. When we got back to Ridgeville with the woman, the people here realized it was inevitable that the Campbells would come. But everybody thought they'd come either alone or with just a few men. And it was agreed with little discussion that we would make a stand. We posted lookouts on three sides of Ridgeville, with small groups of armed men behind them. We ignored the bluff because there is no way into town from up there."

Standing in the doorway, smoking his cigarette and watching the empty street, Edge saw Doc Hunter reappear at the doorway of his office carrying a carpetbag. The tall and distinguished-looking man cast many nervous glances over his shoulder—toward the timber-flanked trail west of town—as he came back down Pine Street, trying not to hurry.

"I ran into the group to the south," Edge said.

"We heard. The shooting spooked one or two of the other forward contingents and they were alarmed into firing at imaginary attackers."

"The two fellers who killed Fred Caxton weren't imaginary, Linn," Edge said.

Hamilton Linn was not aware until now that the shooting to the south of Ridgeville had involved anybody other than Edge. And his face clouded with another frown of fear as more beads of sweat oozed out of his unhealthy-colored skin. But the actor heard the footfalls of Hunter outside and managed to compose himself before the doctor came back into the stable.

"I didn't enjoy that one little bit," Hunter rasped, doing some sweating of his own.

"The horse will appreciate it if you can stop your hands shaking before you start digging for the bullets, Doc," Edge said as Hunter went into the stall with the wounded mare.

"I can take care of my end of the bargain we struck, Edge!" came the response in an even tone, the man's fear already contained as he prepared to undertake a task at which he was expert.

Once in front of a third party, Hamilton Linn slid easily into the part he had been playing in public since returning to Ridgeville. "If two of the Campbells' men were advancing from the south, we must assume others are attempting to reach town secretly elsewhere?"

Edge dropped his cigarette and crushed it out under a heel as the mare whinnied softly.

"You've got that covered, feller," he said, still surveying the street with his glinting blue eyes under the hooded lids. "If that's what's happening and they weren't scared off by the shooting, we'll get fair warning of any more plays like that."

He was still aware of many eyes gazing at him with considerable animosity. If anything, it was stronger now. But not all directed at him, of course. Hamilton Linn was in the livery and he was more responsible for what was happening in this once untroubled town than Edge.

"When they find out they've lost two men, it could spur them to a vengeance attack, Mr. Edge," Linn suggested evenly, but his small eyes pleaded for help.

"Not while Craig Campbell still thinks you have his woman."

"And they all continue to obey the Campbell brothers," Hunter said from the stall.

"That has been a cause for concern from the very start, Mr. Edge," Linn said. He moved to put his back toward the stall where Hunter was working on the mare. To be sure that the doctor could not see the growing look of fear on his face. "The Campbell brothers entered town under a flag of truce to demand the return of Fay Lynch and to state the alternatives. We asked for time to consider and they agreed. But while we and several of the town's leading citizens were meeting in the saloon, we heard from one of our forward lookouts that there had been an argument among the Campbell bunch. And that although the Campbell brothers carried the day, there was a good deal of resentment among those who favored attacking Ridgeville and letting Fay Lynch take her chances."

"Hey, what the hell's goin' on down at JJ's place?" a man roared from the entrance of the Lone Pine Saloon. "Come on up here and let all of us in on it!"

"Crazy fool!" Hamilton Linn rasped.

"He's just scared, like all of us," Hunter growled.

"What did Craig Campbell say when you said he would have his woman back for the money that was taken from the bank?" Edge asked.

The actor shook his head, confusion added to the anxiety on his face. "That's the reason why so many Ridgeville people don't have their hearts in this, Mr. Edge. Campbell maintains nobody from Cloud Pass was responsible for the raid on the bank. And quite a few people halfway believe him."

"Far as Campbell knows, he's telling the truth, feller."

"What!" Linn exclaimed, even his voice now registering his extreme anxiety.

"You mean . . ." Hunter started to ask from the stall.

"You hear me down there at the livery?" the man on the threshold of the saloon bellowed, louder than before. And this time Edge recognized the voice. It was Phil Fry, the lumberman who had placated Jack Quinn at the sawmill office. Now he was using angry bluster to try to mask fear.

But the man who began to shout from an upper-story window of Miss Emma's boardinghouse made no attempt to conceal his true feelings.

154

"Oh, my God! The Campbells are comin', the Campbells are comin'!"

"Are they, mister?" Hunter asked huskily and started out of the stall.

Edge watched the two riders on the trail for a few moments, then said, "It's for real, Doc. But I'd be obliged if you'd keep on with what you're doing with my horse."

"You hear me!" the man in the boardinghouse yelled. "The Campbells are comin'!"

Edge said over the buzz of talk that started all over town, "Sure, but it ain't nothing to make a song and dance about."

Chapter Fourteen

THEY rode slowly, side by side and perhaps three feet apart, Craig Campbell on the left. The lengths of their shadows revealed the fact that there was still something like an hour to go before the noon deadline was reached. But they rode with revolvers in their holsters and rifles in the boots and without a flag of truce.

If there was more talk within the buildings of Ridgeville, it did not carry outside. There was just a brief shuffling of feet as the hidden citizens of the town switched their attention from the livery stable to the Campbells—or, more precisely, to the point on Pine Street where the slow-riding brothers would first come into their field of vision. Then what would have been utter silence descended upon Ridgeville—had not the sounds of the fast-flowing creek and the clop of hooves disturbed it.

Until Edge stepped out of the shaded doorway of the livery, stooping to slide the Winchester out of the saddleboot as he did so. And Hamilton Linn rasped, "What are you doing, man?"

"Same as the doc, feller. Attending to my

business." And under his breath he added, "Hopeful I ain't been in it too long."

He showed himself just as the Campbell brothers rode off the trail and onto the end of Pine Street in front of Harry Bellinger's funeral parlor. Edge was too far away to hear anything that was said, but he saw by the way Craig snapped his head around to look at his brother that Ewan had said something when he caught sight of Edge.

Then both riders faced front again and continued down the street at the same easy pace as before.

Edge, carrying the Winchester in a one-handed grip low down at his left side and with his right hand hanging close to the butt of his holstered Colt, heard fast-moving footfalls behind him. They slowed and from the corner of his eye he saw Hamilton Linn matching pace with him to his left—the actor's hand in the bullet-holed pocket of his duster.

"There comes a time when the playacting has to stop, Mr. Edge," he murmured out of the side of his nearly rigid mouth. "Life is real, life is earnest."

"Like death, feller."

"As Byron said in a vastly different context, Mr. Edge, all tragedies are finished by a death."

The Campbell brothers reached the point where Pine intersected with Douglas Street and Craig reined to a halt. By watching him carefully, Ewan was able to halt his horse at precisely the same time. Edge and Linn arrived at the opposite side of the intersection a few moments later and came to a stop as the half-breed rasped, "This ain't so much a tragedy as a farce seems to me.

157

Matter of who gets caught with their pants down."

"Who are you?" Craig Campbell demanded. His voice was as devoid of emotion as his face.

Ewan tried to remain as inscrutable as his brother and Edge, but could not control a low growl when the half-breed answered flatly, "Friend of a feller you killed the other night."

"I told these people . . ." He waved his right hand to encompass the surrounding buildings and show he knew he was being watched from inside them. ". . . that I know nothin' about the raid on the bank and the killin's."

"Except what my friend told you, feller."

Craig was momentarily confused, then surprised, then impassive again. "You talkin' about John James, mister?"

"You got it."

"Hey, how does he know . . . ?" Ewan Campbell started to ask, but dried up when Craig scowled at him.

"He was up at the pass," Craig said with a nod. "Couple of buddies stickin' together. And you didn't spot him."

"Hell, nobody ever thought there was more than one guy out—"

"It wasn't like that," Edge cut in. He looked directly at Ewan when he said, "It wasn't your fault. Same as it wasn't anybody's fault your whole bunch missed the message a feller named Al Falcon left for you."

"Al Falcon?" Craig snarled, suddenly angry. And within a fraction of a second of lashing out at anything or anybody within range.

But for once—perhaps the only time it ever happened—Ewan was the steadying influence on Craig. "Easy, brother!" the Campbell without the mustache advised. "Falcon ain't hereabouts right now!"

"Craig, Ewan!" Phil Fry yelled from behind the batwings of the saloon entrance.

The usually dominant brother was calm again, but only for a moment. The turbulent emotion aroused within him by the name of Al Falcon was still there, held back by an insecure dam. "Yeah, Fry?" he responded, without shifting his unblinking gaze from the face of the man who had triggered his rage.

"You and your brother ain't got no white rag tied to a rifle this time, Craig. But we given you the benefit of the doubt. You wanna get said what you come to say? Or you gonna draw them six-guns and start blastin'? To hell with the deadline and Fay Lynch?"

Craig Campbell turned his head slowly to the side, looked briefly toward the entrance of the saloon, and spat pointedly into the dust of the intersection. Then he returned his gaze to the face of Edge, raising his right hand off the saddlehorn to level the index finger at Hamilton Linn. "He was the town's mouthpiece the first time. Been any change since then?"

There was a pause during which the actor seemed to pray for somebody to speak in his place. When no one did, he answered, "You may address your remarks to me, sir. And I will be pleased to relay them to anybody not within earshot who needs to know."

Edge heard the scratch of fear only vaguely in the booming tone of Linn.

159

"You talk fancy, mister," Craig said. "And some of us have been gettin' to thinkin' that you might be pullin' somethin' fancy. Like bringin' in a gunfighter. Like this one too shy to say who he is. You are a gunfighter, ain't you, stranger?"

"When I have to be, feller."

"And you had to be—down by the creek awhile ago? When you killed Kendrick and Ed Fletcher?"

"They shot my horse, feller."

"You did not respect the truce!" Linn accused. "You used the time to bring men—"

"And some of them been usin' their times with me, Craig!" a woman shrieked from Miss Emma's boardinghouse. "Seven of the sonsofbitches have had their way with me! And all you can do is yak! Let go of me, you . . . Oh, no! Don't! Please don't . . ."

"Not just a woman. The identifiable voice of a particular woman. Who everybody within earshot except the Campbell brothers knew to be dead. With a single exception, all heads turned in shocked attention toward the shaded stoop of the boardinghouse, where they heard running footfalls accompanied by the shouted, terror-filled pleas. Edge alone kept his attention riveted upon the two Campbells as the door of the boardinghouse was wrenched open, a gunshot exploded, the woman screamed and covered her face with her hands as she crashed down across the threshold.

"But she's dead alread—" Hamilton Linn boomed in disbelief.

Then, for the second time, he was sent sprawling to the ground as the half-breed lunged

160

into him. On this occasion, though, it was Edge who fired the shot as he snarled, "And Jesus Christ was the only one who ever did an encore of that act."

Chapter Fifteen

IT was the half-breed's Winchester that cracked a bullet toward Ewan Campbell, as the faster-on-the-draw brother streaked a hand to reach for his Colt before Elizabeth Miles hit the stoop.

He took it in the chest, left of center, and the impact of the lead tearing through his flesh and into his heart caused him to half-turn in the saddle before he toppled over his bedroll and off the rump of his suddenly spooked mount.

Craig Campbell's rage burst through the veneer of composure he had managed to cloak it in for the past few minutes—but it did not blind him to the percentages. Despite seeing the woman he thought was Fay Lynch blasted to death and part of a second later witnessing at even closer quarters the killing of his brother, he was able to react with great speed, and without panic. He elected to go for cover instead of a gun. For the moment.

He wrenched on the reins to wheel his mount away from the Ewan's rearing horse and spurred the animal to an instant gallop toward the alley between the Lone Pine Saloon and a dry-goods store. He had his Colt clear of the holster midway to his objective and fired it at the first target that came to hand.

It was Phil Fry, who had lunged through the batwing doors of the saloon when Edge triggered the rifle shot—second only to the half-breed in realizing the woman on the boarding house stoop could not be Fay Lynch.

Despite his realization, he was shocked by what had appeared to happen and surprised by his own reaction to the half-breed's shot. The speed with which Craig Campbell turned and raced his horse for cover only disoriented him further.

Because his business was timber, not guns. So he had his rifle aimed at where Craig Campbell had been instead of where he was. While Campbell's Colt was pointed directly at him when the trigger was squeezed. Phil Fry died on his feet with an expression of confusion on his face. The bullet drilled into the center of his forehead, halting the forward momentum of his upper half while his leading leg continued forward. With the result that his feet were brought out from under him and he crashed heavily down on to his back.

The shot that killed the lumberman sounded in unison with one fired by Edge, the half-breed having drawn a dead man's Colt from his holster, thumbed the hammer back, tracked the barrel after Campbell, and squeezed the trigger. All this took less time than was necessary to work the action and fire the Winchester.

Campbell expected to be shot at and he instinctively swayed from side to side in the saddle. Even though Edge had allowed for this, a curse ripped from his bared teeth as his bullet went low and to its left—to smash the glass of the dry-goods store's display window.

Then the mounted man was out of sight, having plunged into the alley. Eddies of rising dust marked his passing.

These explosions of violence took place in the space of a few seconds. No more than five. And in no less time the rage which had powered the curse from deep within Edge was gone. He felt ice-cold in the warmth of the late morning, while everyone around him was seized by fury.

Riders came plunging out of the trees on three sides of Ridgeville and spurred their horses at a full gallop into town. It was the hard men and some of their women. Thieves and killers, starved for the luxuries they'd been unable to enjoy at derelict fort in Cloud Pass. Led to Ridgeville in sure and certain hope of getting free access to everything the town had to offer. Only to be held back after two of their number had been killed. Now they were unable to contain themselves after seeing another of their kind and one of their women—they thought—gunned down.

They came shrieking curses, yelling the battle cries of the Civil War, and firing their guns for cover, for effect, and for sheer pleasure. Soon would have targets to aim at, and they were expert marksmen. As expert as Ewan Campbell had been—and Craig Campbell still was.

And Edge.

The half-breed, his Colt back in his holster and the now cocked Winchester in a two-handed grip across his chest, went into the alley after Campbell. He'd seen the riders on the trail and heard their rage. He'd seen Hamilton Linn scramble up from the ground and start to run toward the boarding house. Where the grinning and uninjured Elizabeth Miles tugged a wig of black hair off her head as she was helped to her feet by a satisfied-looking Miss Emma Roche. And he'd sensed the enmity, which had been like a physical presence in town all morning, suddenly expand. But it was directed with enraged venom at targets other than Edge. Shocked eyes which had failed to see the bullet-shattered corpse of Fred Caxton saw what was left of Phil Fry. One of their kind. And now they would see a mass attack by men of the same kind as the one who blasted the bullet into Fry.

The gunfire of the invaders began to be returned by the defenders.

In the alley between the windowless walls of the saloon and the store Edge and Craig Campbell stood alone. The tall half-breed in damp, wrinkled clothing came to a splayed-legged halt at the front end, teeth still bared and rifle still held in a diagonal line across his chest. While the slightly shorter but more broadly built Campbell remained in his saddle as he wheeled his horse at the other end, the Colt still in his left hand.

There was fifty feet between them, and expert that he was, Campbell knew this was too long a range for a handgun unless his luck was running well. And experts did not rely on luck, he realized, as he recovered from the shock of seeing the half-breed. For it had been his intention to spring a surprise by the sudden about-face. He held still, the Colt low down and aimed at the ground, answering Edge's killer grin with a silent snarl. The half-breed started to walk along the alley.

"You have to wipe out the whole of the Campbell family, huh?" he asked.

"Your brother was faster than me, feller. Had to get him first."

"Poor guy never knew what hit him, you sneaky bastard."

"I did something to make him look the other way?"

Campbell's ruggedly handsome face briefly clouded over with grief, while Edge halted ten feet in front of the black gelding. The horse seemed as unruffled by the gunfire and the shouting of the battle as the two men who shared the relative peace of the narrow alley with him. Then the soundless snarl was back in place on the face of the mounted man. He spoke as if each word tasted sour and he was glad to spit it out of his mouth.

"Fay should have trusted me, mister. She'd still have been alive. And so would Ewan, Phil Fry, and all these people who are getting theirs now."

Riders were galloping along the street; some loose horses, too; and some men on foot. And were intent upon unleashing their fury.

"Was going to pay the ransom, mister." He patted one of his saddlebags with his free hand. "Don't know how much was taken from the bank, but there's a hundred thousand and better on this horse."

Edge nodded. "Your life savings? Not the kind of money you leave lying around when you leave home."

"Not so much left home as moved house, mister. And I reckon we could've done it peaceable if we'd been allowed."

166

"And got back your down payment soon as you had your feet under the table?"

"Only right. Since we didn't rob the bank here. You said something about Al Falcon?"

Edge knew it would soon be time to kill Craig Campbell or die in the attempt. He had moved up close enough for the mounted man to be sure of a killing shot with the handgun. Now, however, before trying for the kill, the man simply wanted to have his curiosity satisfied.

"Old enemy of yours I figure."

"From way back in our Frisco days. Can't be certain who double-crossed who, but Al finished up with his face on the wanted flyers. Hid him out up at the pass last year. Seemed like forgive and forget time. But I figured then he was real jealous of the sweet setup me and Ewan had goin' for us." He spat over the head of his horse and the globule of saliva hit the ground a few feet in front of Edge. "You gonna tell me what you know about him now, mister?"

"That he screwed up your sweet deal. Robbed the town bank after Bill Sheldon told him the right day to do it. Then double-crossed Sheldon in the worst way. Hanged him from a tree on your regular route between the pass and town. But it was dark when you came down and you rode right under him. Didn't see the message that was tied to his body. Boasting about how much smarter he is than a Campbell. Guess he must have meant you, feller."

The battle continued uninterrupted in the streets and buildings of Ridgeville, the raucous noise of the fighting and dying entering the alley where a side issue was being contested. The noise

167

and just a faint odor of gunsmoke. Faint because the pine scent from the surrounding timber quickly overpowered it. And the stink of fear did not carry this far.

"Ewan never claimed to be smart, mister," Craig Campbell said as he and Edge locked gazes. "Just the fastest there is in a *fair* gunfight. As a lot of men found out in the last second of their lives. Me, I'm nowhere near as fast. But I'm smarter than Al Falcon and I'm smarter than you, you bas . . . no, Leo, he's mine!"

The calm voice suddenly rose half an octave and the steely gaze shifted from the bristle face of Edge to the entrance of the alley behind him. The Colt in his left hand swung upward.

Edge had a brief glimpse of Oliver Strange on the saloon roof. He did not believe the redheaded man named Leo was behind him. He dropped to a half-crouch and brought the Winchester around to the aim when he heard a gunshot and felt the grin become a scowl on his features. He wondered why he did not feel the thud and then the searing heat of a bullet entering his flesh.

But Campbell's Colt was unfired in his hand. Then the fingers opened and allowed the revolver to drop to the ground. And Edge saw it was the man astride the gelding who had taken the bullet. It had drilled a blood-blossoming hole in his chest.

Still down in the crouch, Edge whirled to make sure that Craig Campbell had not tried to work the oldest trick in the book and was stunned to see that the man named Leo was standing in the mouth of the alley. In his hand was the single-shot Spencer he had fired at the back of Edge a fraction of a second after the half-breed bobbed out of the line of the bullet—which had instead found the heart of Campbell.

Edge heard Campbell's corpse thud to the ground. The horse snorted. Leo recovered from the shock of killing the wrong man, hurled down the rifle, and clawed for the Colt in his holster.

Once more Edge took first pressure against the trigger of his rifle. The grin began to spread across his face again. Only to freeze back into the scowl when the sharpshooting Marybelle Melton leaned out of the doorway of the drugstore across the street and triggered a bullet from her long-barrel Colt. It took Leo in the center of the back and sent him sprawling along with alley before his own gun was out of the holster. Edge controlled a fresh wave of white-hot fury, contenting himself with shaking his fist and looking daggers at the female sharpshooter.

Marybelle Melton looked surprised, then disappointed, and scurried back inside the drugstore. Her smile of pleasure had abruptly disappeared when the man she had hoped would now forgive her for having shot a gun from his hand was instead glaring at her with depthless hatred.

But then he succeeded in making his emotions as ice cold as the look in his glittering eyes as he moved to the mouth of the alley. The sounds of battle were diminishing. Which meant that the time for proving something to himself was running out.

He stepped out from the alley with the rifle canted to his shoulder and his gun hand hanging close to the holstered Colt. He was risking his life on his own terms because unless he could prove himself, he was likely to die elsewhere on some-body else's.

But it was too late.

The shooting abruptly ceased and the attackers were in full retreat, astride horses and on foot, across the intersection. Too anxious to escape the wrath of the people of Ridgeville to waste precious seconds with covering fire.

And some paid dearly for this haste, meeting their end in pools of blood on Pine and Douglas streets at high noon in this Montana town. The blades of broadaxes, the sharply pointed heads of pickaxes, and even the honed metal of four-foot hafted falling axes sunk into their flesh with sickening thuds that seemed to sound in awesome isolation from the thud of galloping hooves and the screams of terror and agony.

These workaday tools of the lumberman's trade were hurled down from rooftops or out of doorways with great skill and accuracy, driving with massive strength deep into backs, chests, bellies, and even necks. Often the blood was stemmed by the tight fit of the metal in the wound—until the victims fell and rolled and the axes and pickaroons were torn free. Then great gushing torrents of dark crimson splashed across the street surface.

Men and women alike had fallen and were still falling victim to this lethal barrage, which was as effective and more terrifying than any firearms could have been. Those who succeeded in escaping the axes had to run or gallop their mounts through a hail of cross fire that exploded from both sides of the upper length of Pine Street. And many made it through, for the people of Ridgeville were not experts with guns. Nor, with the single exception of Marybelle Melton, were the Linn Players.

Edge watched with a bleak-eyed look but took no part in this picking off of the remnants of the Campbell bunch. The final shot was fired after the last man to stagger out of town. The bullet missed the intended target and the man made it safely into the cover of the trees to one side of the trail.

Gunsmoke drifted and soon disintegrated in the air of early afternoon. But its taint clung to the atmosphere and masked the stink of fear that emanated from those attackers and defenders who were badly wounded enough to sense the approach of death. The cries of the wounded and the wails of the bereaved continued for a long time, but reached the ears of Edge in muted form once he turned his back on the body-littered and bloodstained intersection and pushed through the batwing doors of the saloon.

Which was empty.

He checked the clock on the wall behind the bar to see if it really was past midday before he took a bottle of rye and a glass off a shelf and started to drink. And to smoke. Both slowly, but constantly.

While he reflected upon the violent events of the recent past and his part in them, he decided that he would have played a different role had he been younger. But, he asked himself, so what? Circumstances altered things in the lives of everybody. And no matter how different a man considered himself to be, all had much in common.

Certainly getting old was an inescapable penalty for staying alive. And there were inevitable consequences of the aging process. Like getting testy and getting forgetful. For a man who lived like Edge such consequences could only mean that the sands of his living were starting to run out fast. And lately he had allowed dangerous anger to trigger many of his actions. Even worse, there had been a glaring example of forgetfulness: when he had overlooked the need to test-fire the gun he had confiscated from a dead man. He himself could have died when he discovered in a gunfight that the Colt fired low and to the left.

Getting softhearted was also a sign of too many years gone by, he guessed. And he had been that, too. Toward John James. Even toward Hamilton Linn—when he shoved the actor out of the line of fire at a time when gunning down both Campbell brothers should have been his sole concern.

But forgetting to try out a dead man's gun until he needed it in a kill or be killed situation . . . that was what irked him most. And threatened to arouse fresh anger. At the back of his mind lurked a nagging worry that there was something else he had forgotten.

The sounds outside became even less intrusive as the day wore on. Then the town was quiet—mournfully so—as the light got dimmer and the air chillier.

Standing at the counter, the rifle resting across its top, Edge made the bottle last all afternoon, so he was not the least drunk when he heard the batwings swing. He did not sense any threat so he remained facing the counter with a cigarette angled from a corner of his mouth and a half-filled glass between both hands against his chest.

"They say that drinking alone is bad for a

172

man," Doc Hunter said as he came across the saloon and went behind the bar.

He sounded very weary and when Edge looked at him in the light of a lamp he lit, the half-breed saw the Ridgeville doctor was near to exhaustion. But he could also tell that the blood that stained his clothing and smudged his gaunt face was not his own. "Or there's another school of thought," he replied as Hunter took down a bottle and poured himself a rye, "that says drinking is all that makes being alone bearable. Among other things."

The doctor replaced the bottle on the shelf with grim-faced resolution—determined to ration himself to just the one shot. "You're not that kind, Edge." He raised his glass. "Here's to all survivors."

"My horse going to be one of those?"

"Give her a week to mend and you can ride her. Just finished treating her. After patching up twenty townspeople and five men who came with the Campbells. One of them won't last through the night is my guess. And maybe three of my regular patients will die. Brings the total of Ridgeville's loss to sixteen. Which includes Moss Tracy, Edge. But somebody will inherit this place." He pointedly took out some coins from a pants pocket and placed a few cents on the countertop beside his empty glass.

"You happen to know if a feller named Donovan from the pass was killed, Doc?" Edge asked as Hunter came out from behind the bar and headed for the batwings.

"Yeah, he was killed. Knew him from treating

him for boils one time. Something special about him?"

"Owed him for a bottle of whiskey I took to help JJ on his way out."

"Reckon you can forget it." Hunter paused with a hand on the top of the door. "Yeah, and forget what you've had here, too. Folks are in two minds about you and those theatricals right now. Take them a time to get over their grief, I guess, but when they do, they ought to feel grateful to you for giving them back their pride.

"I feel that way already—knowing I won't ever again have to lance the boils of a psychopathic killer. Or treat a man who broke his arm escaping from a posse after robbing a stage. Or lots of other things that used to stick in my craw.

"I've already told the group of actors something of the kind. And you played no small part in bringing things to a head. Night to you."

Just as Hunter went from the saloon, Edge recalled that he had not told anyone in town—except for Craig Campbell—that Bill Sheldon would not be bringing replacement payroll money from Casper. But he knew this was not the cause of the nagging worry at the back of his mind.

"An extremely large part, I'd say," Hamilton Linn boomed as he pushed through the batwings before they had finished flapping from Hunter's exit. "Had you not responded so quickly and skillfully to the excellent but rather reckless piece of drama staged by dear Elizabeth, there is no telling what the out-come might have been."

"No sense worrying about what might have happened, feller," Edge growled without turning around.

174

"I come to bid you farewell, sir. And to thank you for perhaps saving my life. Who knows, if you had not knocked me to the ground once again, I—"

"Like I just said, Linn—"

"Of course, of course. I felt I had to say it, though. Today has been a triumph in one way, in another it has been a failure. The stolen money was not recovered and the Linn Players must press on to a new engagement in a community which can afford to pay the admission price for our entertainment."

"Like they say, the show must go on," Edge murmured, and the important memory clicked to the forefront of his mind.

"Precisely."

The actor's boot leather scraped on the floor as he turned and the batwings flapped again. Edge finished his drink, set the glass on the countertop, and picked up the Winchester to go across the saloon, dimly lit by the single lamp Hunter had illuminated.

From the threshold he looked diagonally across the intersection, which had been cleared of corpses but still showed many bloodstains, to where a covered wagon with an elaborately and vividly painted canvas was parked, a four-horse team in the traces.

The elderly Clarence Gowan was up on the seat, the reins in his hands. Grouped at the rear were the girlishly good-looking Oliver Strange, the untrusting Henry Maguire, the plain Susie Chase, and the boy sharpshooter, Marybelle Melton. The man-hating Elizabeth Miles was already aboard, leaning out over the tailgate to look, like the others, up the steps of the boardinghouse to the lighted hallway. There, in silhouette against the lamp glow, the duster-coated Hamilton Linn was taking his effusive leave of Miss Emma Roche.

There was an eager tension in the attitues of the actors and actresses near or aboard the wagon. And this tension suddenly seemed to be transmitted to Linn—for, although nothing was called to him, he abruptly bowed to the elderly spinster, turned, and hurried down the steps. He headed for the wagon with the intention of climbing up on the high seat beside Gowan.

But before he did so, he handed up a pair of bulky saddlebags which the man holding the reins accepted with relief. He did so at the same time as Maguire, sensing watching eyes, shot a glance over his shoulder and recognized Edge standing between the half-open batwings.

"Shit," he snarled, "it's that hard-nosed Mex-looking cowboy again, Ham!"

It was enough to get him killed, calling Edge a Mex. But he had to wait his turn. For Clarence Gowan had his shotgun on the seat beside him. He dropped the saddlebags, snatched it up, and thumbed back the hammers as he swung it around to aim across the intersection. The group at the rear whirled and yelled for Elizabeth Miles to toss their guns out.

The half-breed remained where he was as he brought the barrel of the Winchester down from his shoulder and thudded the stockplate into it. He placed the first bullet into the forehead of the old man on the wagon seat just as he aligned the sights of his shotgun on the saloon doorway. Next he stepped out of the doorway and raked the re-

176

peater along the garishly painted side of the wagon as he worked the lever action. He located the crack shot Marybelle Melton as she made to level her long barrel Colt in a double-handed grip. Shot her in the chest, drilling the bullet under the bullet under the gun and her outstretched arms.

He was clear of the saloon now, in the same moonlight that bathed the wagon and the Linn Players. He planted his feet firmly on the intersection to explode a bullet into the side of Oliver Strange's neck—as the girlish-looking young man snatched his Winchester from the hands of Elizabeth Miles.

The sight of arterial blood gushing from the flesh of the toppling youngster drove Maguire into an insane rage. And he lunged forward as he fired his Spencer, as if he needed to make physical contact with Edge.

"My Pa was a *Mexcian!*" the half-breed rasped as he squeezed his trigger a split second after Maguire fired his shot.

One bullet smashed a window of the Lone Pine Saloon. The other tunneled into the left eye of Henry Maguire.

The plain-faced Susie Chase had half climbed and been half hauled into the rear of the wagon by Elizabeth Miles. Now both women began to scream as they peered out of the rig and saw the limp corpses of three of their number sprawled in a heap below the tailgate. The high-pitched sounds they made drowned out the many shouted questions from battle-weary townspeople who feared the survivors from Cloud Pass had returned—as well as whatever the shocked Hamilton

177

Linn was shrieking from his position of retreat on the boardinghouse stoop.

Edge had raked the Winchester muzzle back along the wagon's side with cool speed to locate the actor. He saw he had his hand in his duster pocket, but knew the tiny gun he carried posed no danger over such a range. And now he altered the aim of the rifle again as he began a slow advance across the intersection. While he methodically fired the gun and pumped its action, sending a stream of bullets through the canvas side of wagon until the magazine was empty. The final shellcase fell to the ground at his side.

The utter silence which followed was almost painful to the eardrums.

Edge broke it with his footfalls as he went to the rear of the wagon and, careful to avoid stepping on any of the dead, glanced in over the tailgate. He saw the two women clasped to each other in a deathly embrace, their dresses marred by many dark stains. The stink of something that was a natural reaction to terror was heavy in the air under the bullet-holed canvas.

"What in heaven's name have you done?" Hamilton Linn croaked. He stood with his back pressed hard against the closed door of the boarding house.

Edge moved around the rear of the wagon and advanced on him, the empty Winchester canted to his left shoulder and his hand close to the holstered Colt, his narrowed and glittering eyes fastened tenaciously upon the gaunt and ashen face of the actor. He was aware that Linn still had his left hand in the bullet-holed pocket of his duster.

"Figure I've just made a not so old man very

happy, feller," Edge replied as he halted, six feet in front of Linn, once again within range of a small but lethal gun.

"Are you mad?"

"Maybe I was going a little crazy when I couldn't get the chance to prove to myself I'm as good as I need to be." He paused to purse his lips and then then added softly: "Still."

"At killing innocent people you provoked into—"

"More of you than me, which evened the odds. One question for you. In case you figure to try to kill me."

The actor gulped and his eyes moved back and forth in their sockets, sweeping over the stunned and silent townspeople who had gathered around the wagon. "Olly Strange was on the roof of the saloon. He heard you and Campbell talking in the alley. When he told us about the hundred thousand in the saddlebags on that loose horse we all agreed to . . ."

An angry murmuring had started among the audience Hamilton Linn would rather not have had. And he found himself unable to go on with what he was saying because of the constriction that fear placed around his throat.

But the crowd was not concerned with the actor for the moment. The townspeople were only interested in the pair of saddlebags that the towering Geroge had dragged down from the seat where Gowan had dropped them when he reached for his shotgun.

"Wasn't my question, feller," Edge said. "Who took my money?"

"Elizabeth!" he blurted and Edge accepted this as the truth. For the slightly built actor had proven many times that he was not a coward and would not now have hidden behind the skirts of a dead woman. "That was entirely her idea, sir. I swear it. She told us about it when we got back to town. She was concerned that we could not manage on our own against the men at the pass. So she took your money in the hope you would agree to be hired to—"

"Obliged," the half-breed interrupted. "She still have it?"

"Hey, mister, you can take what you're owed outa this," George invited in high excitement. He opened the saddlebags and held them out for his fellow citizens to see the bills stuffed inside.

"No need," Linn said across the fresh buzz of eager talk. "If you'll look under the straw in the corner of the stall where she nursed you, you'll find the money. She never really took it, you see. Just hid it."

"Obliged again."

"We aren't thieves really, you know!" Linn blurted and swept his worried eyes over the audience again. "We didn't take Mr. Edge's money. And the money in those saddlebags doesn't belong to anybody else here! The man who had it is dead and it wasn't truly his anyway! My entire troupe was slaughtered for doing nothing that was in any way criminal. It was a matter of finders—"

"The hell with that, mister!" Jack Quinn cut in. "You and your bunch knew the whole town was stole from and yet you was gonna take—"

"Yeah, that's right!" a woman accused.

"Get aboard your wagon and haul yourself and

your dead outa our town, mister!" a lumberman snarled.

Edge had turned away as the crowd moved in closer around the wagon, some of them coming between himself and the frightened actor. Harry Bellinger, the town mortician, was among these. The half-breed addressed his word to him. "Seems I won't need that casket after all, feller."

"If you did, you'd be at the end of a long waitin' list, sir."

Linn jerked his hand out of his pocket, empty, suddenly aware that the half-breed was no longer a threat to him. And that the small gun he had been gripping was useless against the mob that threatened him.

"Mr. Edge!" he called. "These people look like they might . . . Where are you going, Mr. Edge?"

The man cowered, terrified of the crowd which was babbling with discontent and rage until the voice of Doc Hunter was heard. Suddenly all murmuring ceased. "Just do as you were told and leave town, sir!" Hunter commanded.

"Yeah, get your show on the road!" Jack Quinn snarled.

"I should say so!" Miss Emma called down from an upper-story window.

"Going, feller?" Edge murmured as he halted his movement toward the stable. He watched lumbermen loading the dead players into the rear of the wagon and decided to wait until tomorrow to tell the people that Bill Sheldon would never return to Ridgeville. "North is Canada and that don't appeal to me too much right now. Not far west is the ocean and I don't swim so well. Come up here from the south . . ."

He paused to take out the makings and start to roll a cigarette as the morose-looking actor without a company climbed up on to the wagon seat. Then he concluded: "My horse needs to rest up for a while. So could be, next week, east Linn."

More bestselling western adventure from Pinnacle, America's #1 series publisher. Over 8 million copies of EDGE in print!

CELEBRATING 10 YEARS IN PRINT
AND OVER 22 MILLION COPIES SOLD!